# Lancaster Cemetery
# Garrard County
# Kentucky
# Interment Dates & Locations
# 1995-2010

ISBN 978-0-9818351-1-2
Published by Etcetera Publishing LLC — Fort Worth, TX
Printed in the United States of America
First Edition

Please visit www.PersonalTouchGenealogy.com
to order this book or see Order Form on page 65.

# Lancaster Cemetery
# Garrard County
# Kentucky
## Interment Dates & Locations
# 1995-2010

by

## J. L. Dickson

In association with

**Personal Touch Genealogy**
www.PersonalTouchGenealogy.com

*and*

ETC
ETCETERA
PUBLISHING

www.GenealogyBookPublisher.com

A **receiving vault** is typically an underground crypt or above-ground building built within a cemetery, with the purpose of storing the bodies of deceased persons in winter months when the ground is too frozen to dig a permanent grave. Modern mechanical all-weather digging tools have mostly replaced the need for such receiving vaults in today's cemeteries.

The receiving vault above is no longer used, however, is still standing. This vault was built in 1897, and is located near the front of the Lancaster Cemetery in Lancaster, Kentucky.

# ACKNOWLEDGMENTS

The information in this book was extracted from the
Lancaster Cemetery sexton records.

Every attempt was made to ensure the information herein is
as it was logged in those records.

Lancaster cemetery started in 1857; however, there are
indications that some who had died before 1857
may have been moved there.

In this book the interment dates are listed, however this
can be a great help in genealogical research, just knowing
that the person in question is, in fact, buried there.

*This book covers only 1995-2010.*

# Explanation of the Information in This Book

The listing contains the following information:

| | |
|---|---|
| Name | Person that is deceased |
| Sec | Section number in Lancaster Cemetery |
| Plot | Lot number within section |
| Grave | Place of grave within lot |
| Interment date | Date of burial |
| Director | Name of funeral director who was in charge of burial |

Any fields that are blank were blank in the sexton's records.

In the few that are listed with two grave numbers, the cremains were either buried between the two said graves, or divided between the two graves.

| Name | Sec | Lot | Grave | Interment Date | Director |
|---|---|---|---|---|---|
| Abee Dorothy | 21 | 24 | 14 | 14-May-1996 | Ramsey |
| Abee Steve | 21 | 24 | 7 | 28-Feb-2005 | Spurlin |
| Ackinson Evaree | 29A | 14 | 6 | 31-Oct-1998 | Ramsey |
| Adams Addie | 23 | 28 | 10 | 2-Feb-2004 | Spurlin |
| Adams B. Lance | 24 | 4 | 2 | 20-Jan-2007 | Spurlin |
| Adams Beulah | 29A | 132 | 7 | 13-Nov-2003 | Ramsey |
| Adams Daniel | 34 | 36 | 6 | 25-Sep-2001 | Spurlin |
| Adams Edith | 29 | 38 | 3 | 22-Jun-1999 | Ramsey |
| Adams Ernest | 29A | 132 | 8 | 1-Jun-1999 | Ramsey |
| Adams Ethel | 23 | 28 | 3 | 28-Feb-1996 | Ramsey |
| Adams G. Lillie | 30 | 130 | 7 | 5-May-1995 | Ramsey |
| Adams Giovanna | 33 | 26 | 5 | 12-Jan-1995 | Ramsey |
| Adams J. Thomas | 30 | 138 | 4 | 25-Jan-2005 | McNight |
| Adams Joetta | 21 | 2 | 15 | 3-Feb-2003 | Spurlin |
| Adams Lucas | 33 | 42 | 8 | 18-Aug-2008 | Ramsey |
| Adams P. James | 29A | 76 | 6 | 11-Jan-2003 | Ramsey |
| Adams Timothy | 34 | 3 | 2 | 26-Aug-2006 | Spurlin |
| Adkison Charles | 22 | 21 | 4 | 11-Nov-1999 | Spurlin |
| Adkison Jimmie | 30 | 54 | 1 | 4-Sep-2007 | Ramsey |
| Aldridge Helena | 22 | 2 | 11 | 17-Apr-1997 | Ramsey |
| Aldridge L. Sidney | 21 | 2 | 19 | 7-Jul-2007 | Milward |
| Aldridge Rena | 30 | 113 | 1 | 21-Sep-1998 | Spurlin |
| Allen Frank | 23 | 32 | 9 | 15-Nov-2007 | Ramsey |
| Allen Joyce | 31 | 25 | 5 | 10-Nov-2008 | Spurlin |
| Altman P. Anne | 26 | 7 | 2 | 20-Dec-2007 | Lange |
| Amon Rosella | 30 | 81 | 7 | 27-Dec-1997 | Ramsey |
| Amstutz John | 29A | 83 | 2 | 1-Aug-1997 | Ramsey |
| Amstutz John | 29A | 83 | 1 | 12-Feb-2004 | Ramsey |

| Name | Sec | Lot | Grave | Interment Date | Director |
|---|---|---|---|---|---|
| Amstutz Naylor Dorothy | 29A | 82 | 4 | 29-Jun-1995 | Ramsey |
| Anderson C. John | 19 | 11 | 15 | 17-Nov-2009 | Pruitt |
| Anderson Clarence | 30 | 77 | 8 | 12-Sep-1996 | Fox |
| Anderson Ida | 19 | 11 | 14 | 24-Nov-2007 | Ramsey |
| Anderson Jewell | 33 | 13 | 1 | 25-May-2009 | Spurlin |
| Anderson K. Jennie | 27 | 2 | 13 | 15-Nov-2007 | Kerr Bros |
| Anderson Ralph | 33 | 44 | 4 | 17-Sep-1999 | Ramsey |
| Anderson Shelby | 20 | 5 | 7 | 15-Oct-2007 | Spurlin |
| Antle Sutton Clara | 27 | 36 | 9 | 12-Dec-2002 | Ramsey |
| Arnett M. Ada | 34 | 5 | 6 | 10-Apr-2003 | Somerset |
| Arnold A. Margaret | 23 | 23 | 14 | 22-Jun-2010 | Ramsey |
| Arnold Benjamin | 3 | 34 | 10 | 23-Nov-1999 | |
| Arnold C. John | 32 | 5 | 6 | 8-Sep-2010 | Spurlin |
| Arnold Colby | 23 | 23 | 15 | 16-Feb-2002 | Ramsey |
| Arnold Coy (Sr.) | 20 | 8 | 8 | 2-Jun-2006 | Spurlin |
| Arnold Delores | 20 | 8 | 7 | 5-Oct-1995 | |
| Arnold Edd | 4 | 26 | 16 | 22-Jan-2000 | Ramsey |
| Arnold James (Sr.) | 34 | 15 | 8 | 22-Nov-2005 | Spurlin |
| Arnold Janice | 34 | 64 | 1 | 31-Oct-2007 | Ramsey |
| Arnold Kathy | 34 | 15 | 6 | 28-Nov-2009 | Ramsey |
| Arnold Minnie | 4 | 26 | 15 | 18-Jan-2002 | Ramsey |
| Arnold Patricia | 34 | 7 | 3 | 9-Jan-2006 | Spurlin |
| Arnold Ray Frances | 25 | 18 | 1 | 21-Aug-1995 | Ramsey |
| Arnold T. Alexander | 23 | 31 | 5 | 28-Nov-2008 | Ramsey |
| Bailey Cox Nellie | 9 | 26 | 3 | 24-Oct-1995 | Ramsey |
| Bailey Jack | 30 | 79 | 8 | 15-Nov-1996 | Spurlin |
| Bailey R. Ray | 32 | 12 | 6 | 3-May-2010 | Ramsey |

| Name | Sec | Lot | Grave | Interment Date | Director |
|------|-----|-----|-------|----------------|----------|
| Baker Anna | 24 | 13 | 15 | 13-Jul-2005 | Ramsey |
| Baker Carl | 25 | 11 | 10 | 18-May-2005 | Spurlin |
| Baker Coleman | 30 | 140 | 2 | 18-Feb-2006 | Combs |
| Baker Earl | 27 | 15 | 15 | 11-Apr-1996 | Bowling |
| Baker Edith | 33 | 18 | 5 | 18-Dec-2010 | Ramsey |
| Baker Laura | 30 | 140 | 1 | 12-Apr-2008 | Combs |
| Baker Louellyn | 29 | 24 | 8 | 16-Feb-1998 | Fox |
| Baker Olivette | 29 | 13 | 16 | 2-Oct-1995 | Ramsey |
| Baker Sarah | 25 | 11 | 9 | 22-Oct-2003 | Spurlin |
| Baker Susie | 21 | 22 | 3 | 3-Jun-1998 | Ramsey |
| Baker Thomas | 33 | 46 | 6 | 16-Oct-1996 | Ramsey |
| Baker W. J. | 21 | 1 | 8 | 19-Dec-2000 | Oldman |
| Ball Betty | 16 | 9 | 15 | 29-Aug-2008 | Ramsey |
| Ball Cristine | 20 | 31 | 14 | 21-Sep-1996 | Ramsey |
| Ball James | 29A | 91 | 2 | 24-Dec-1998 | Ramsey |
| Ball Louis | 23 | 7 | 4 | 17-Nov-2009 | Ramsey |
| Ball Russell | 34 | 16 | 2 | 27-Jun-2009 | Ramsey |
| Ballard Andrea | 33 | 61 | 3 | 19-Jun-2004 | Ramsey |
| Ballard Dora | 33 | 29 | 7 | 16-Feb-2009 | Spurlin |
| Ballard Georgia | 25 | 38 | 6 | 17-Jun-2002 | Spurlin |
| Ballard Jesse | 30 | 129 | 2 | 29-Oct-1999 | Ramsey |
| Ballard Leeds | 32 | 15 | 4 | 14-Feb-2006 | Spurlin |
| Ballard Makl | 32 | 15 | 7 | 17-Jan-2009 | Spurlin |
| Ballard Patricia | 17 | 31 | 12 | 9-Sep-2010 | Spurlin |
| Ballard Ruth | 32 | 15 | 3 | 29-Jun-2010 | Spurlin |
| Bannister Patricia | 29 | 32 | 4 | 5-Dec-2001 | Kerr Bros |
| Bannister S. Sue | 29 | 32 | | 20-Oct-2006 | Kerr Bros |
| Barker Charles | 16 | 47 | 8 | 23-Aug-2004 | |

| Name | Sec | Lot | Grave | Interment Date | Director |
|---|---|---|---|---|---|
| Barker Dorothy | 16 | 36 | 9 | 15-Aug-2000 | Ramsey |
| Barker E. Anna | 16 | 36 | 7 | 18-Jan-2007 | Spurlin |
| Barker Jacqueline | 19 | 21 | 10 | 11-Aug-2004 | Ramsey |
| Barker Mamie | 21 | 25 | 9 | 11-Aug-2003 | Spurlin |
| Barker Paul | 16 | 36 | 156 | 24-Nov-1998 | Ramsey |
| Barnes C. Agnes | 11 | 4 | 15 | 16-Jan-2006 | Ramsey |
| Barnes Charles | 30 | 122 | 2 | 24-Dec-2008 | Ramsey |
| Barnes Freda | 25 | 36 | 10 | 2-Nov-2004 | Stith |
| Barnes L. Poyper | 30 | 122 | 5&6 | 16-Jul-2010 | Spurlin |
| Barnes Michelle | 30 | 39 | 5 | 6-Oct-1999 | Spurlin |
| Barnes Oneeta | 30 | 122 | 1 | 11-Mar-2009 | Ramsey |
| Barnett George | 3 | 24 | 5 | 25-Feb-2005 | Spurlin |
| Barton Charles | 30 | 176 | 6 | 15-Oct-2002 | Ramsey |
| Bauer Pamela | 32 | 26 | 3 | 18-Apr-2006 | Ramsey |
| Bayse Donald | 33 | 37 | 2 | 25-Aug-1995 | Ramsey |
| Beck Hagen Dora | 25 | 37 | 15 | 27-Dec-2000 | Fox |
| Begley Clyde | 34 | 24 | 2 | 2-Feb-2005 | Ramsey |
| Bell B. Beverly | 11 | 11 | 4 | 19-May-2007 | Spurlin |
| Berkley William | 6 | 8 | 16 | 13-Jan-1998 | Ramsey |
| Berry Fred | 29A | 95 | 2 | 4-Nov-1998 | Fox |
| Berryman Velma | 30 | 58 | 1 | 25-Apr-2001 | Milward |
| Beszly McPhearson Dorothy | 30 | 136 | 5 | 28-Dec-1999 | Ramsey |
| Bisher Valerie | 34 | 57 | 5 | 28-Aug-2007 | Spurlin |
| Bishop Ester | 11 | 1 | 5 | 15-Apr-2006 | Fern Creek |
| Bishop W. John | 11 | 1 | 6 | 7-Apr-2005 | Fern Creek |
| Black Elvin | 29 | 7 | 16 | 22-Aug-1995 | Ramsey |
| Black Jeff | 27 | 22 | 4 | 8-Sep-2007 | Ramsey |

| Name | Sec | Lot | Grave | Interment Date | Director |
|---|---|---|---|---|---|
| Black Mattie | 29 | 7 | 13 | 21-Nov-2001 | Spurlin |
| Black William | 29A | 79 | 3 | 22-Aug-2002 | Ramsey |
| Blaydis Sallie | 30 | 153 | 5 | 29-Apr-2002 | Ramsey |
| Bogie Daisey | 25 | 3 | 3 | 24-Jun-2010 | Fox |
| Bolton Clyde | 31 | 24 | 2 | 20-Sep-2007 | Spurlin |
| Bolton Dean | 32 | 39 | 4 | 13-Jun-2009 | Spurlin |
| Bolton E. Sarah | 30 | 166 | 5 | 28-Oct-2006 | Ramsey |
| Bolton James | 11 | 43 | 10 | 15-Apr-2002 | Ramsey |
| Bolton Jimmy | 27 | 32 | 7 | 30-May-1996 | Ramsey |
| Bolton Mae | 30 | 16 | 5 | 2-Oct-2010 | Ramsey |
| Bourne Adolph | 9 | 34 | 11 | 4-Mar-1996 | Ramsey |
| Bourne Charles | 21 | 21 | 16 | 10-Nov-2007 | Ramsey |
| Bourne Elam Gladys | 9 | 34 | | 1-Sep-2008 | Ramsey |
| Bourne Fannie | 16 | 9 | 1 | 10-Jun-2004 | Spurlin |
| Bourne Irene | 21 | 21 | 7 | 17-Sep-2002 | Ramsey |
| Bourne J. Margaret | 19 | 8 | 2 | 26-May-2005 | Stith |
| Bourne Julian | 21 | 21 | 8 | 26-Feb-1996 | Ramsey |
| Bourne K. James | 32 | 28 | 4 | 13-Jan-2007 | Spurlin |
| Bourne Lillie | 28 | 17 | 9 | 27-Feb-2001 | Ramsey |
| Bourne Mary | 32 | 28 | 3 | 5-Mar-2007 | Spurlin |
| Bourne Samuel | 21 | 21 | 15 | 26-Jul-2010 | Ramsey |
| Bradley Warren | 30 | 95 | 6 | 22-Jul-2004 | Ramsey |
| Brandenburg Dorothy | 21 | 1 | 10 | 19-Jan-2009 | Lakes |
| Branham Doris | 34 | 8 | 8 | 19-Dec-2006 | Spurlin |
| Brashear William | 9 | 8 | 8 | 14-Mar-1997 | McClellan |
| Bratton G. R. | 12 | 23 | 16 | 29-Oct-1996 | Ramsey |
| Bratton Nancy | 12 | 23 | 6 | 13-Aug-2005 | Ramsey |
| Bray William | 30 | 141 | 4 | 3-Jul-1996 | Ramsey |

| Name | Sec | Lot | Grave | Interment Date | Director |
|---|---|---|---|---|---|
| Brickey Lee Mary | 30 | 30 | 1 | 8-Jul-2002 | Ramsey |
| Brickey Melissa | 33 | 34 | 5 | 17-Aug-1995 | Ramsey |
| Brickey William | 27 | 12 | 15 | 4-Aug-2003 | Ramsey |
| Bridges Milton | 33 | 29 | 4 | 25-Jan-1996 | Preston Pruitt |
| Brigmon Clay Robert | 15 | 6 | 4 | 1-Aug-2001 | Kerr Bros |
| Brigmon Mary | 15 | 6 | 3 | 25-Feb-2003 | Kerr Bros |
| Brim James | 23 | 32 | 16 | 24-Jan-2005 | McKinney |
| Broaddus Annetta | 30 | 61 | 1 | 15-Nov-1999 | Spurlin |
| Broaddus Clarence | 29 | 14 | 15 | 29-Nov-1996 | Ramsey |
| Broaddus Elveree | 30 | 68 | 6 | 19-Aug-1999 | Ramsey |
| Broaddus Felda | 30 | 25 | 7 | 5-Feb-2003 | Ramsey |
| Broaddus Florence | 20 | 49 | 9 | 19-Aug-2009 | Spurlin |
| Broaddus James | 29A | 124 | 7 | 20-Jan-2004 | Spurlin |
| Broaddus Joe | 30 | 25 | 8 | 16-Jun-1997 | Ramsey |
| Broaddus Katherine | 5 | 24 | 9 | 3-Dec-2001 | Ramsey |
| Broaddus Lula | 24 | 32 | 12 | 9-Apr-1996 | Ramsey |
| Broaddus N. Mary | 29A | 124 | 5 | 9-Oct-2002 | Spurlin |
| Broadus Christine | 30 | 132 | 5 | 21-Jun-2007 | Newcomer |
| Broadus Eratus | 30 | 61 | 2 | 31-Jan-1997 | Spurlin |
| Broadus Hubert | 29A | 93 | 2 | 23-Feb-1999 | Ramsey |
| Broadus Ida | 29 | 28 | 10 | 17-Nov-1999 | Ramsey |
| Broadus M. Wayne | 26 | 20 | 8 | 28-May-2001 | Spurlin |
| Broadus M. Winfred | 30 | 147 | 6 | 8-Jul-2008 | Woodline |
| Broadus Margaree | 29A | 112 | 4 | 15-Feb-1997 | Oldman |
| Broadus Pauline | 26 | 20 | 1 | 9-Mar-2009 | Spurlin |
| Broadus Walker | 5 | 24 | 8 | 1-Jun-1999 | Ramsey |
| Brock Cora | 32 | 11 | 3 | 22-Oct-2004 | Ramsey |

| Name | Sec | Lot | Grave | Interment Date | Director |
|---|---|---|---|---|---|
| Broddus N. Ashley | 25 | 33 | 6 | 21-Mar-2008 | Ramsey |
| Brodell Sally | 33 | 27 | 4 | 20-Nov-1998 | Ramsey |
| Brodell Thomas | 33 | 43 | 2 | 15-Aug-1997 | Ramsey |
| Brogli Agnes | 16 | 43 | 7 | 30-May-2007 | Ramsey |
| Brogli Geneva | 16 | 40 | 1 | 12-Aug-1997 | Ramsey |
| Broglie T. William | 16 | 40 | 2 | 31-Dec-2010 | Spurlin |
| Broglie Vernon | 16 | 43 | 6 | 24-May-2010 | Ramsey |
| Brooks Gladys | 29A | 70 | 1 | 3-Aug-1999 | Ramsey |
| Brooks Lee Mary | 30 | 174 | 5 | 12-Jan-2009 | Spurlin |
| Broughton Brian | 29 | 8 | 12 | 25-Jan-1996 | Ramsey |
| Brown Clifford | 30 | 47 | 2 | 3-Oct-2008 | Spurlin |
| Brown Elizabeth | 23 | 33 | 10 | 7-Nov-1996 | Ramsey |
| Brown R. James | 30 | 102 | 4 | 25-Apr-2003 | Spurlin |
| Brown Ruby | 19 | 20 | 10 | 19-Jan-2004 | Dowell & Martin |
| Brown Vivian | 30 | 28 | 3 | 22-Aug-1995 | Ramsey |
| Browning Frank | 30 | 140 | 6 | 16-Sep-2003 | Ramsey |
| Browning Lillian | 30 | 140 | 5 | 22-May-2007 | Ramsey |
| Browning Roger | 33 | 33 | 6 | 18-Jul-1995 | Ramsey |
| Bruner B. Lenora | 20 | 11 | 2 | 14-Oct-1999 | Spurlin |
| Bryant Billie | 34 | 10 | 1 | 2-Jul-2008 | Spurlin |
| Burdette Emma | 24 | 5 | 4 | 9-Dec-2004 | Ramsey |
| Burdette O'Rear | 33 | 27 | 4 | 15-Aug-1997 | Ramsey |
| Burdette Rhoda | 29A | 60 | 8 | 6-Nov-1998 | Ramsey |
| Burge McClellan | 17 | 10 | 8 | 20-Jan-1999 | McNight |
| Burke Helen | 30 | 23 | 7 | 20-May-1996 | Mt. Sterling |
| Burke Polmer | 34 | 22 | 6 | 16-Jun-2006 | |
| Burkhart Burley | 33 | 21 | 3 | 19-Nov-1997 | Ramsey |

| Name | Sec | Lot | Grave | Interment Date | Director |
|---|---|---|---|---|---|
| Burkhart Cora | 20 | 40 | 12 | 22-Mar-1995 | Ramsey |
| Burkhart Eula | 33 | 21 | 2 | 19-Jun-2000 | Ramsey |
| Burnside Allen | 1 | 12 | 17 | 6-Feb-2008 | Fox |
| Burnside Grace | 30 | 57 | 3 | 5-Feb-2002 | Spurlin |
| Burnside Jacob | 30 | 57 | 4 | 4-Aug-2004 | Spurlin |
| Burton May Helen | 17 | 7 | 14 | 18-Dec-1998 | Ramsey |
| Cain Audrey | 33 | 49 | 2 | 30-Apr-2003 | Spurlin |
| Cain J. Shelby | 33 | 44 | 7 | 9-Aug-2005 | Spurlin |
| Caldwell Walter (Jr.) | 30 | 119 | 2 | 31-Jan-2009 | Ramsey |
| Calhoun David | 29 | 3 | 9 | 16-Jan-1999 | McNight |
| Callicoat Margery | 30 | 60 | 7 | 10-Jul-1996 | Ramsey |
| Camel Betty | 33 | 28 | 6 | 4-Aug-2004 | Ramsey |
| Camel Lula | 30 | 104 | 7 | 6-Dec-2004 | Ramsey |
| Canter Howard | 30 | 114 | 5 | 4-Aug-1997 | Ramsey |
| Carmichael Lenora | 20 | 2 | 8 | 27-Mar-2009 | |
| Carpenter Lillian | 33 | 15 | 7 | 15-Feb-2005 | Ramsey |
| Carpenter William | 12 | 43 | 14 | 24-Apr-2003 | Ramsey |
| Carrier Ann Mary | 21 | 10 | 2 | 2-Oct-2000 | Spurlin |
| Carrier Cynthia | 25 | 6 | 9 | 2-Mar-2004 | Ramsey |
| Carrier Elisha | 25 | 6 | 11 | 23-Apr-1997 | Ramsey |
| Carrier Jimmy | 34 | 39 | 4 | 2-Jun-2009 | Spurlin |
| Carrier Leonard | 29 | 30 | 16 | 11-Feb-2008 | Ramsey |
| Carrier Lewis | 34 | 7 | 6 | 23-Dec-2002 | Ramsey |
| Carrier Nellie | 33 | 36 | 5 | 23-Apr-2010 | Spurlin |
| Carrier Otis | 30 | 16 | 8 | 13-Oct-2006 | Spurlin |
| Carrier Ruby | 34 | 7 | 5 | 11-May-2007 | Ramsey |
| Carrier Shelly | 34 | 4 | 5 | 22-Jul-2005 | Ramsey |
| Carroll N. Gladys | 33 | 58 | 5 | 22-Jan-2001 | Spurlin |

| Name | Sec | Lot | Grave | Interment Date | Director |
|---|---|---|---|---|---|
| Carter G. Baker | 30 | 67 | 2 | 24-May-2008 | Morris & Hislope |
| Carter Inis | 30 | 67 | 1 | 17-Sep-2008 | Morris & Hislope |
| Carter Mary | 29A | 64 | 2 | 17-Jan-2002 | Spurlin |
| Carter William | 29A | 64 | 3 | 6-Feb-2007 | Spurlin |
| Casey Farrie | 30 | 59 | 1 | 26-May-1998 | Ramsey |
| Casey H. William | 16 | 19 | 8 | 6-Dec-1997 | Ramsey |
| Casey N. Gladys | 32 | 26 | 5 | 16-Sep-2008 | Spurlin |
| Cason Gladys | 9 | 33 | 11 | 22-Mar-1999 | Milward |
| Caudill R. Paul | 30 | 152 | 1 | 25-Nov-2000 | Fox |
| Chadwell Corb | 16 | 43 | 12 | 31-Mar-1998 | Ramsey |
| Chadwell Hazel | 12 | 17 | 15 | 16-Jul-2001 | Spurlin |
| Chadwell Paul | 16 | 43 | 10 | 24-Mar-2008 | Spurlin |
| Chambers Meadow | 23 | 16 | 10 | 31-Jul-2003 | Spurlin |
| Chance Gilbert | 20 | 12 | 15 | 19-Jan-2001 | Ramsey |
| Chance Virginia | 20 | 12 | 14 | 29-Nov-2010 | Ramsey |
| Chappell Thomas | 2 | 29 | 7 | 5-May-1998 | Ramsey |
| Christopher Belle Nora | 20 | 50 | 11 | 5-Jul-2007 | Ramsey |
| Clark Anna | 26 | 25 | 10 | 6-Sep-1995 | Ramsey |
| Clark B. Howard | 17 | 12 | 3 | 1-May-2006 | Johnson |
| Clark David | 28 | 12 | 11 | 7-Jul-2008 | Ramsey |
| Clark Elizabeth | 28 | 10 | 15 | 16-May-2001 | Spurlin |
| Clark Geneva | 30 | 57 | 7 | 27-May-1999 | Ramsey |
| Clark Helen | 21 | 14 | 10 | 26-Aug-1997 | Spurlin |
| Clark Homer | 20 | 39 | 11 | 18-Jan-1997 | Ramsey |
| Clark Jo Betty | 28 | 12 | 9 | 15-Mar-2006 | Ramsey |
| Clark Nancy | 24 | 33 | 9 | 19-Aug-1995 | Ramsey |

| Name | Sec | Lot | Grave | Interment Date | Director |
|---|---|---|---|---|---|
| Clark Orville | 28 | 10 | 16 | 20-Jul-2007 | Spurlin |
| Clark Paul | 9 | 35 | 15 | 11-Jan-2000 | Spurlin |
| Clark Reba | 30 | 99 | 3 | 5-Jan-2008 | Spurlin |
| Clark Ruth | 29A | 53 | 7 | 9-Nov-1996 | Ramsey |
| Clark Thelma | 29A | 98 | 1 | 5-Jan-2002 | Ramsey |
| Clark William | 29A | 53 | 8 | 5-Aug-2004 | Ramsey |
| Cochran Ray Georgia | 18 | 18 | 15 | 13-Aug-2001 | Preston Pruitt |
| Coffey Burford | 7 | 21 | 16 | 26-Oct-2004 | Ramsey |
| Coffey Delores | 33 | 22 | 4 | 28-Dec-1995 | Ramsey |
| Coffey Elsie | 7 | 21 | 15 | 6-Sep-1999 | Ramsey |
| Coffey Leander | 30 | 126 | 6 | 23-Mar-2002 | Spurlin |
| Coffey R. Mary | 33 | 5 | 5 | 29-Jan-2007 | Ramsey |
| Coffey Stella | 27 | 19 | 7 | 22-Mar-2000 | Ramsey |
| Coffey Winfred | 23 | 14 | 10 | 18-Jan-2001 | Spurlin |
| Cole Robert II | 27 | 4 | 11 | 14-Jun-2010 | Ramsey |
| Coleman Lillie | 36 | 22 | 5 | 30-Sep-2010 | Ramsey |
| Collett Jimmie | 23 | 21 | 6 | 30-Jul-1999 | Parrot & Ramsey |
| Collett Luther | 20 | 51 | 13 | 23-Nov-1996 | Ramsey |
| Collett Robert | 30 | 142 | 6 | 6-Jun-2009 | Spurlin |
| Collett William | 33 | 57 | 6 | 2-Nov-1998 | Ramsey |
| Collette Jinger | 23 | 21 | 5 | 23-Mar-2010 | Parrott & Ramsey |
| Colson Margaret | 33 | 36 | 2 | 20-Apr-2010 | Combs |
| Colson Z. Anna | 29A | 122 | 7 | 28-Nov-2009 | Kerr Bros |
| Colyer Ellen Lou | 18 | 21 | 11 | 4-Feb-1995 | Ramsey |
| Colyer William | 18 | 21 | 9 | 15-Jan-1996 | Ramsey |
| Combs Ernest | 30 | 120 | 2 | 30-Oct-2010 | Spurlin |

| Name | Sec | Lot | Grave | Interment Date | Director |
|---|---|---|---|---|---|
| Combs Evelyn | 30 | 120 | 1 | 19-Feb-2003 | Spurlin |
| Combs Grace | 30 | 120 | 5 | 8-Jun-2002 | Spurlin |
| Comley Margaret | 30 | 71 | 7 | 14-Jan-2006 | Ramsey |
| Compton Jerry | 23 | 17 | 16 | 27-Sep-2004 | Ramsey |
| Compton Mary | 21 | 26 | 16 | 6-Sep-2004 | Ramsey |
| Conn Bertha | 26 | 3 | 6 | 27-Jan-2005 | Ramsey |
| Conn Carl | 27 | 28 | 3 | 2-Apr-1997 | Ramsey |
| Conn Edwin | 29A | 104 | 2 | 26-Sep-2000 | Ramsey |
| Conn Jewell | 29A | 104 | 1 | 12-Jul-1999 | Ramsey |
| Conn Sallie | 18 | 34 | 1 | 18-Sep-1997 | Dalbert & Woodruff |
| Conn Susie | 21 | 27 | 9 | 25-Mar-1996 | Elliston |
| Conn Tillie | 27 | 28 | 4 | 10-Jul-1995 | Ramsey |
| Cook Leona | 12 | 44 | 12 | 16-Nov-2006 | Preston Pruitt |
| Cooms Willa | 16 | 46 | 15 | 15-Jul-1996 | Arnette & Steele |
| Cooten Virginia | 25 | 17 | 15 | 6-Jan-2001 | Ramsey |
| Cormny Josephine | 9 | 1 | 7 | 31-Jul-1998 | Ramsey |
| Cornelius Cecil | 30 | 170 | 1 | 31-Dec-2007 | Spurlin |
| Cornelius G. Bobby | 36 | 16 | 8 | 24-Jul-2010 | Ramsey |
| Cotton Evelyn | 29A | 77 | 5 | 14-Apr-2004 | Ramsey |
| Cotton Owsley | 27 | 6 | 15 | 2-Apr-2002 | Ramsey |
| Cotton Ralph | 29A | 78 | 5 | 6-Jul-2009 | Spurlin |
| Cotton W. John | 25 | 17 | 5 | 17-Sep-2002 | Preston Pruitt |
| Courtney & Thuis (infant) | 33 | 60 | 1 | 5-Nov-1999 | Spurlin |
| Cox Doxie | 30 | 100 | 7 | 4-Nov-2002 | Spurlin |

| Name | Sec | Lot | Grave | Interment Date | Director |
|---|---|---|---|---|---|
| Cox Earl | 25 | 8 | 8 | 8-Jul-1995 | Preston Pruitt |
| Cox Estelle | 30 | 101 | 5 | 7-Sep-1995 | Ramsey |
| Cox Hubert | 30 | 100 | 8 | 23-May-1997 | Spurlin |
| Cox J. Hester | 25 | 8 | 7 | 24-Nov-2007 | Preston Pruitt |
| Coyle Jamin | 30 | 24 | 2 | 9-Sep-2010 | Spurlin |
| Craft Katherine | 25 | 17 | 2 | 21-Sep-2000 | Ramsey |
| Craft Thomas (Jr.) | 25 | 17 | 1 | 24-Sep-2008 | Ramsey |
| Crane Dororthy | 34 | 28 | 2 | 11-Feb-2002 | Ramsey |
| Cranmer Edward | 4 | 26 | 14 | 2-Jul-2004 | Ramsey |
| Creech Lincoln | 33 | 26 | 4 | 7-Oct-1995 | Ramsey |
| Creech Ruby | 33 | 26 | 3 | 23-Aug-1995 | Ramsey |
| Creech W. Charles | 30 | 122 | 2 | 24-Dec-2008 | Spurlin |
| Crenshaw Ozella | 27 | 20 | 11 | 13-Oct-2003 | Spurlin |
| Crews Etta Georgia | 24 | 11 | 9 | 20-Apr-1998 | Spurlin |
| Crisicillis Carl | 16 | 31 | 11 | 31-Aug-1998 | Ramsey |
| Crisicillis Stella | 16 | 31 | 10 | 10-Aug-1998 | Ramsey |
| Crouch Kenneth | 23 | 2 | 2 | 19-Apr-2008 | Stith |
| Croushorn Earl Robert | 16 | 54 | 8 | 24-Sep-1998 | Ramsey |
| Crow Lucritia | 23 | 41 | 13 | 1-Jun-2001 | Stith |
| Crow Peachie | 12 | 44 | 3 | 17-Feb-1997 | Ramsey |
| Crutcher Margaret | 30 | 141 | 6 | 18-Feb-2005 | Ramsey |
| Crutcher Winnie | 29 | 3 | 14 | 7-Oct-1999 | Turpin |
| Crutchfield Joel | 34 | 30 | 4 | 30-Mar-2010 | Spurlin |
| Cunningham Ralph | 27 | 18 | 3 | 2-Aug-2002 | Ramsey |
| Cupp Cora | 33 | 23 | 1 | 24-Mar-1999 | Ramsey |
| Cupp Moses | 33 | 22 | 2 | 26-Nov-2002 | Ramsey |

| Name | Sec | Lot | Grave | Interment Date | Director |
|------|-----|-----|-------|----------------|----------|
| Curtis Gordon | 25 | 13 | 3 | 10-Jul-2007 | Ramsey |
| Curtis Mary | 25 | 13 | 15 | 10-May-1997 | Ramsey |
| Curtisinger Martha | 33 | 59 | 7 | 29-May-2000 | Spurlin |
| Dailey Allen Mack | 30 | 117 | 4 | 23-May-1995 | Ramsey |
| Dailey Beatrice | 21 | 28 | 2 | 28-May-2001 | Ramsey |
| Dailey Bobby | 30 | 90 | 3 | 22-Jul-2000 | Ramsey |
| Dailey C. W. | 33 | 22 | 6 | 26-Dec-2001 | Ramsey |
| Dailey Flora | 33 | 22 | 5 | 11-May-2000 | Ramsey |
| Dailey P. Sean | 21 | 28 | 1 | 3-Jul-2002 | Ramsey |
| Dailey Pinia | 34 | 58 | 1 | 13-Jun-2009 | Ramsey |
| Dailey Sally | 29A | 114 | 1 | 18-Aug-1998 | Ramsey |
| Dailey Shirley | 30 | 90 | 4 | 30-Jun-2008 | Ramsey |
| Daley James | 29A | 105 | 4 | 27-Jul-2009 | Spurlin |
| Daly James | 29A | 105 | 8 | 31-May-2003 | Spurlin |
| Daly Sam | 30 | 141 | 8 | 1-Apr-2000 | Ramsey |
| Daniel Bill | 14 | 12 | 3 | 12-Apr-1997 | Ramsey |
| David Aronld | 33 | 54 | 8 | 11-Oct-1999 | Ramsey |
| David Mathews Betty | 21 | 23 | 8 | 24-Aug-1999 | Spurlin |
| Davis Alvin | 33 | 25 | 8 | 23-Jun-2007 | Ramsey |
| Davis Ambers | 21 | 10 | 16 | 25-May-2000 | Ramsey |
| Davis Annabelle | 21 | 10 | 13 | 16-Nov-2006 | Ramsey |
| Davis Carl | 30 | 3 | 8 | 8-Sep-2001 | Ramsey |
| Davis Charlotte | 29A | 142 | 1 | 29-Nov-2002 | Ramsey |
| Davis Christine | 5 | 29 | 9 | 15-Aug-2002 | Owens |
| Davis Cotha | 21 | 10 | 6 | 19-Apr-2008 | Best & West |
| Davis Elizabeth | 29 | 4 | 15 | 30-Apr-2004 | Spurlin |
| Davis Florence | 20 | 43A | 9 | 24-May-1997 | Ramsey |
| Davis Frances Willie | 21 | 10 | 15 | 2-Sep-2000 | Ramsey |

| Name | Sec | Lot | Grave | Interment Date | Director |
|------|-----|-----|-------|----------------|----------|
| Davis Johnetta | 25 | 3 | 6 | 18-Nov-1999 | Ramsey |
| Davis Mae Ida | 30 | 140 | 4 | 14-Jun-2001 | Ramsey |
| Davis Morris | 30 | 114 | 2 | 20-Dec-1999 | Ramsey |
| Davis Norman | 11 | 31 | 8 | 18-Feb-2002 | Ramsey |
| Davis Otha | 30 | 24 | 4 | 22-Jan-1996 | Ramsey |
| Davis Roland | 29 | 22 | 12 | 28-Jan-1995 | Ramsey |
| Davis Sue | 30 | 3 | 7 | 31-Aug-2001 | Ramsey |
| Davis Willard | 21 | 10 | 7 | 26-Jun-2002 | Best & West |
| Day Joyce | 30 | 82 | 7 | 5-Jun-2003 | Alexander |
| Day Mary | 33 | 33 | 8 | 27-Nov-1995 | Ramsey |
| Day Versie | 30 | 109 | 2 | 20-Jul-1998 | Ramsey |
| Dean Anna | 30 | 102 | 5 | 28-Jul-2009 | Ramsey |
| Dean C. Robert | 34 | 13 | 8 | 12-Dec-2006 | Spurlin |
| DeBard Betty | 31 | 6 | 1 | 10-May-2006 | Spurlin |
| Denington S. Patsy | 30 | 145 | 1 | 13-Feb-2007 | Ramsey |
| Dennis Annabelle | 28 | 21 | 9 | 11-May-2004 | Spurlin |
| Dennis Bertha | 33 | 20 | 5 | 31-Oct-2001 | Ramsey |
| Dennis Carrie | 16 | 52 | 2 | 25-Sep-2004 | Ramsey |
| Dennis Flonnie | 28 | 21 | 4 | 28-Aug-2000 | Ramsey |
| Dennis R. J. | 28 | 21 | 12 | 23-Oct-2007 | Spurlin |
| Dennis Ruby | 28 | 21 | 10 | 27-Jun-2001 | Ramsey |
| Dennis Stanley | 28 | 21 | 11 | 17-Jun-1998 | Ramsey |
| Denniston Lorraine | 25 | 39 | 11 | 20-May-1997 | Ramsey |
| Denny Joetta | 12 | 9 | 13 | 26-Feb-2004 | Ramsey |
| Denny Thurman | 30 | 155 | 2 | 16-Feb-2001 | Ramsey |
| Denny Virginia | 30 | 84 | 4 | 17-Jun-2010 | Spurlin |
| Denny Willie | 12 | 9 | 14 | 17-Apr-1997 | Ramsey |
| Denton Debbie | 33 | 41 | 3 | 2-Nov-2001 | Ramsey |

| Name | Sec | Lot | Grave | Interment Date | Director |
|------|-----|-----|-------|----------------|----------|
| Deshon Helen | 24 | 21 | 2 | 29-Jun-1998 | Spurlin |
| Deshon Margaret | 29A | 80 | 7 | 26-Dec-2001 | Spurlin |
| Dietrich A. William | 30 | 42 | 2 | 13-Jun-2003 | Spurlin |
| Dietrich B. Harold | 29 | 29 | 15 | 2-Apr-2005 | Spurlin |
| Dillon Sue | 12 | 23 | 9 | 13-Apr-1999 | Ramsey |
| Doe Jane (Unknown) | 20 | 2 | 10 | 16-Sep-2008 | Spurlin |
| Dollin Billy | 33 | 51 | 2 | 12-Apr-2008 | Ramsey |
| Dollins Betty | 27 | 14 | 9 | 6-Jan-2007 | Ramsey |
| Dollins James | 29 | 38 | 15 | 17-Oct-2003 | Ramsey |
| Doody Louise | 29 | 11 | 3 | 30-Aug-2003 | Ramsey |
| Doody Sylvester | 29 | 11 | 4 | 27-Apr-2002 | Spurlin |
| Doolin Ann | 33 | 51 | 1 | 18-Mar-1998 | Ramsey |
| Doolin Lucille | 18 | 3 | 10 | 20-Mar-2008 | Ramsey |
| Doolin M. Flora | 26 | 12 | 6 | 1-Jan-2004 | Ramsey |
| Doolin Roberta | 26 | 12 | 1 | 8-Oct-2003 | Spurlin |
| Doolin Wayne | 26 | 12 | 2 | 13-Jul-2007 | Spurlin |
| Dorton Bertha | 29A | 75 | 7 | 13-May-2010 | Ramsey |
| Dorton Herbert | 29A | 75 | 8 | 5-Jan-1999 | Ramsey |
| Doty B. John | 22 | 12 | 14 | 22-Feb-2005 | Ramsey |
| Doty William | 17 | 13 | 11 | 17-Feb-1998 | Pruitt |
| Douglas Catherine | 16 | 32 | 12 | 28-Dec-1995 | Ramsey |
| Dowd Helen | 7 | 17 | 1 | 28-Nov-1998 | Ramsey |
| Dudderer Dorothy | 26 | 22 | 14 | 4-Mar-2010 | Milward |
| Duggins Louise | 30 | 179 | 1 | 31-Jul-2004 | Ramsey |
| Duggins Mae Ola | 30 | 48 | 7 | 25-Feb-1995 | Ramsey |
| Duggins Mary | 30 | 148 | 1 | 13-Mar-1995 | Ramsey |
| Duncan Cecil | 29A | 88 | 8 | 6-Oct-2001 | Spurlin |
| Duncan Clay | 28 | 2 | 10 | 9-Feb-2004 | Vaughn |

| Name | Sec | Lot | Grave | Interment Date | Director |
|---|---|---|---|---|---|
| Duncan Helen | 19 | 18 | 1 | 23-Dec-2006 | Ramsey |
| Duncan Sadie | 29A | 88 | 77 | 10-Jan-2004 | Spurlin |
| Duncan Vertie | 23 | 36 | 2 | 16-May-1995 | Ramsey |
| Dunn Christine | 23 | 10 | 7 | 5-May-1999 | Ramsey |
| Dunn Jimmy | 33 | 28 | 3 | 21-Feb-2007 | Ramsey |
| Dunn Katherine | 23 | 36 | 11 | 17-Dec-2007 | Ransdell |
| Dunn Nynter | 14 | 21 | 8 | 22-Jun-2009 | Clark |
| Dunn R. Charles | 14 | 21 | 16 | 17-Sep-2010 | Milward |
| Durham Bobby | 32 | 40 | 6 | 16-Oct-2008 | Ramsey |
| Durham Herman | 30 | 156 | 6 | 23-Feb-2008 | Ramsey |
| Durham J. Betty | 27 | 25 | 5 | 8-Oct-2005 | Spurlin |
| Durham Mildred | 30 | 156 | 5 | 15-May-1995 | Ramsey |
| Durham Robert | 27 | 25 | 6 | 14-Mar-2009 | Spurlin |
| Durham Sam | 29A | 56 | 8 | 11-May-2005 | Ramsey |
| Duvall Raymond | 30 | 30 | 8 | 3-Nov-1999 | McNight |
| Eades Bobby | 23 | 34 | 8 | 25-Apr-1997 | Preston Pruitt |
| Eads R. James | 25 | 39 | 10 | 31-Dec-2005 | Ramsey |
| Eagle W. Delbert | 16 | 46 | 11 | 18-Jan-2010 | Spurlin |
| Eason Allene | 29A | 69 | 5 | 25-Mar-1996 | Mills |
| Eason Hancel | 30 | 39 | 8 | 26-Jan-1995 | Ramsey |
| East Allan | 9 | 33 | 16 | 10-Jul-2006 | Ramsey |
| East Bernice | 9 | 33 | 14 | 29-Nov-2008 | Ramsey |
| East Billey | 30 | 169 | 4 | 19-Nov-1996 | Ramsey |
| East D. J. | 30 | 161 | 4 | 14-Oct-2008 | Ramsey |
| East Robert | 23 | 13 | 2 | 27-Nov-2007 | Spurlin |
| East Thomas | 9 | 33 | 6 | 5-Aug-2010 | Ramsey |
| Easton Wesley | 29A | 69 | 6 | 12-Sep-1995 | Doan & Mills |

| Name | Sec | Lot | Grave | Interment Date | Director |
|---|---|---|---|---|---|
| Eden Virginia | 11 | 43 | 11 | 28-Oct-2010 | Spurlin |
| Edgington Charles | 23 | 33 | 4 | 15-Jun-1999 | Ramsey |
| Edgington Emma | 29A | 54 | 5 | 26-May-2003 | Spurlin |
| Edgington Henry | 33 | 8 | 2 | 5-Mar-1999 | Spurlin |
| Edgington James | 29A | 54 | 6 | 12-Jun-2006 | Spurlin |
| Edgington Joe | 30 | 179 | 4 | 27-Jan-1995 | Ramsey |
| Edwards Arnold | 17 | 25 | 3 | 19-Oct-1995 | Ramsey |
| Edwards Hazel | 17 | 25 | 14 | 28-Oct-2002 | Ramsey |
| Edwards Irene | 30 | 112 | 5 | 24-May-2001 | Ramsey |
| Edwards Kaye | 34 | 8 | 4 | 28-Feb-2003 | Ramsey |
| Edwards Marshall | 30 | 94 | 6 | 19-Sep-2007 | Ramsey |
| Elam L. John | 30 | 12 | 1 | 6-Nov-2008 | Ramsey |
| Elam Levi | 29A | 108 | 3 | 22-Apr-1998 | Spurlin |
| Elam Malinda | 30 | 11 | 3 | 8-Dec-2000 | Ramsey |
| Elkin Carlton (Ms.) | 3 | 19 | 12 | 11-Jan-2007 | Ratterman |
| Elkin Marylyn | 5 | 26 | 1 | 21-Jul-2010 | Ramsey |
| Elliott Della | 22 | 5 | 6 | 16-Jan-2006 | Wright |
| Elliott Dunlap | 22 | 7 | 13 | 5-Jun-1995 | Ramsey |
| Elliott Katherine | 22 | 7 | 12 | 17-Jun-2005 | Stith |
| Ellis Charles | 24 | 6 | 5 | 12-Sep-1998 | Ramsey |
| Ellis Gustava | 33 | 56 | 3 | 4-May-2010 | Ramsey |
| Ellis Ruth | 24 | 6 | 6 | 25-Oct-1995 | Ramsey |
| Ellis Stanley | 32 | 19 | 8 | 30-Jan-2002 | Ramsey |
| Engle Cora | 21 | 19 | 6 | 4-Aug-1995 | Ramsey |
| Engle Mary | 20 | 32 | 14 | 8-Mar-2002 | |
| Enyweiler Agnes | 33 | 39 | 3 | 29-Mar-2004 | Ramsey |
| Estes Belle Edna | 20 | 62 | 7 | 20-May-2006 | Ramsey |
| Estes Cynthia | 27 | 20 | 7 | 2-Aug-2006 | Ramsey |

| Name | Sec | Lot | Grave | Interment Date | Director |
|---|---|---|---|---|---|
| Estes Hobert | 27 | 20 | 8 | 26-Aug-1995 | Ramsey |
| Estes Judy | 25 | 36 | 7 | 16-Nov-2005 | Ramsey |
| Estridge Lucile | 16 | 27 | 2 | 28-Nov-2001 | Ramsey |
| Evans J. Jesse (Rev) | 33 | 52 | 7 | 11-Oct-2000 | Ramsey |
| Evans Lucille | 19 | 6 | 12 | 4-Sep-1998 | Ramsey |
| Eversole J. William | 34 | 46 | 5 | 3-Jan-2005 | Ramsey |
| Fathergill Arbutus | 12 | 2 | 14 | 7-Apr-2010 | Ramsey |
| Feldman Andrew | 29 | 36 | 3 | 3-Jan-2007 | Spurlin |
| Feldman Barbara | 29 | 36 | 12 | 24-Nov-1999 | Ramsey |
| Feldman Robert | 29 | 36 | 4 | 18-May-2010 | Spurlin |
| Ferrell Dorothy | 2 | 22 | 12 | 14-Apr-2003 | Ramsey |
| Ferring Virginia | 23 | 4 | 2 | 16-May-2007 | Spurlin |
| Figgins Flora | 25 | 33 | 1 | 12-Nov-2009 | Ramsey |
| Fisher Geneva | 11 | 8 | 15 | 5-Aug-2010 | Ramsey |
| Flemming O. Maggie | 29A | 109 | 3 | 24-Jan-2003 | McNight |
| Fletcher Irene | 26 | 21 | 1 | 6-Sep-2007 | McNight |
| Fletcher L. Robert | 24 | 1 | 7 | 5-May-1995 | Ramsey |
| Fletcher S. Evelyn | 24 | 1 | 6 | 2-Dec-2010 | Ramsey |
| Floyd Vickie | 32 | 5 | 3 | 18-Oct-2004 | Ramsey |
| Foley D. Lucille | 30 | 67 | 5 | 8-May-2010 | Spurlin |
| Foley Earl | 30 | 67 | 6 | 28-Mar-1997 | Ramsey |
| Foley Paul | 29 | 25 | 11 | 25-Jan-2000 | Ramsey |
| Folger Gerald | 21 | 9 | 7 | 29-May-1995 | Ramsey |
| Forks S. Ercelle | 13 | 15 | 12 | 24-Sep-2002 | Ramsey |
| Foster Anna | 18 | 39 | 9 | 24-Nov-1995 | Ramsey |
| Fothergill Earl | 12 | 34 | 12 | 26-Feb-2002 | Ramsey |
| Fothergill Olaf | 21 | 17 | 14 | 18-Apr-2003 | Ramsey |
| Frances George | 33 | 27 | 2 | 23-May-1996 | Ramsey |

| Name | Sec | Lot | Grave | Interment Date | Director |
|------|-----|-----|-------|----------------|----------|
| Franklin Sadie | 34 | 1 | 5 | 22-Sep-2001 | Fox |
| Frey Lucille | 30 | 110 | 4 | 7-Aug-2007 | Ramsey |
| Friend D. Ella | 33 | 43 | 7 | 25-May-2009 | Ramsey |
| Friend Eva | 33 | 37 | 3 | 10-May-2005 | Ramsey |
| Friend Hubert | 33 | 43 | 8 | 27-Aug-1997 | Ramsey |
| Friend Sam | 33 | 37 | 4 | 23-Nov-1996 | Ramsey |
| Fryman Douglas | 29A | 72 | 1 | 20-Oct-2000 | Milward |
| Fulk Grace | 24 | 8 | 11 | 7-Jun-1997 | Ramsey |
| Fulk Paul | 24 | 8 | 10 | 1-Sep-1998 | Ramsey |
| Fyhe Leo | 30 | 60 | 2 | 26-Aug-2002 | Ramsey |
| Gaffney C. William | 33 | 45 | 4 | 19-Nov-2010 | |
| Gaffney Harrison | 20 | 29 | 11 | 16-Mar-2002 | Spurlin |
| Gaffney Margaret | 33 | 45 | 3 | 27-Oct-2008 | Spurlin |
| Gaffney Mary | 20 | 29 | 12 | 16-Jul-1996 | Ramsey |
| Gains Charles | 30 | 55 | 8 | 8-Apr-1999 | Ramsey |
| Gains W. George | 30 | 134 | 5 | 11-Apr-1997 | Ramsey |
| Gains Wilbur | 32 | 8 | 4 | 27-Jan-1998 | Ramsey |
| Gallagher Jewell | 27 | 16 | 10 | 9-Oct-1995 | Ramsey |
| Gallagher Perpie | 27 | 16 | 9 | 30-Sep-1996 | Ramsey |
| Gambel Susan | 32 | 17 | 5 | 27-Jan-2010 | Ramsey |
| Gardner Helen | 34 | 46 | 4 | 5-Jan-2005 | Spurlin |
| Garner Seth | 34 | 25 | 5 | 28-Oct-2002 | Ramsey |
| Gary H. Herbert | 21 | 13 | 1 | 22-Mar-2010 | Ramsey |
| Gaskin Ann | 20 | 32 | 10 | 1-Oct-2005 | Ramsey |
| Gaskin Delmar | 20 | 32 | 1 | 16-May-2006 | Ramsey |
| Gastineau Frances | 25 | 25 | 7 | 3-Feb-2001 | Ramsey |
| Gastineau James | 33 | 7 | 8 | 27-Jul-1998 | Spurlin |
| Gastineau Nell | 23 | 39 | 14 | 30-Dec-1996 | Royatity |

| Name | Sec | Lot | Grave | Interment Date | Director |
|---|---|---|---|---|---|
| Gastineau Robert | 25 | 25 | 8 | 21-Feb-2007 | Spurlin |
| Gastineau W. Christopher | 34 | 14 | 3 | 15-Dec-2005 | Spurlin |
| Gay Bobby | 22 | 14 | 8 | 22-Apr-2005 | Spurlin |
| Gay Clyde | 22 | 14 | 2 | 5-May-2000 | Spurlin |
| Gay Jessie | 29A | 139 | 1 | 14-May-2002 | Ramsey |
| Gay Nora | 21 | 13 | 9 | 2-Jun-2003 | Spurlin |
| Gay William | 30 | 25 | 4 | 30-Nov-2000 | Lakes |
| Genaw Juanita | 21 | 4 | 9 | 29-Sep-2001 | Combs |
| Gerlach Ann | 16 | 13 | 4 | 9-Oct-1995 | Ramsey |
| Gerlach Samuel | 16 | 34 | 2 | 27-Mar-2009 | Ramsey |
| Gibson Arnold | 33 | 34 | 4 | 7-Oct-1999 | Preston Pruitt |
| Gibson Dorothy | 30 | 168 | 5 | 20-Jul-1996 | Ramsey |
| Gibson L. Mary | 27 | 17 | 1 | 8-Sep-2008 | Ramsey |
| Gifford C. Jeremy | 36 | 10 | 4 | 23-Nov-2010 | Spurlin |
| Gifford James | 33 | 33 | 3 | 13-Oct-2009 | Ramsey |
| Gifford Laura | 33 | 33 | 4 | 3-Oct-1997 | Ramsey |
| Gilbert Rebecca | 30 | 7 | 7 | 18-Mar-2004 | Ramsey |
| Gill Edna | 2 | 12 | 15 | 11-Nov-2005 | Ramsey |
| Gilliam Cindy | 11 | 36 | 1 | 25-Nov-2002 | Ramsey |
| Gilliam Homer | 34 | 8 | 4 | 28-Feb-2003 | Spurlin |
| Gilliam Kenneth | 34 | 39 | 1 | 30-Jan-2003 | Ramsey |
| Gillian Clyde | 32 | 41 | 6 | 21-Sep-2010 | Ware |
| Gillian G. William | 34 | 32 | 2 | 5-Aug-2005 | Ramsey |
| Gillian Lou Sallie | 18 | 28 | 1 | 18-Jul-1997 | Ramsey |
| Gillman Frances | 29A | 61 | 3 | 9-Aug-2000 | Ramsey |
| Giunchigiani Blanch | 27 | 18 | 15 | 15-Feb-2001 | Ratterman |

| Name | Sec | Lot | Grave | Interment Date | Director |
|---|---|---|---|---|---|
| Givens James | 29 | 6 | 12 | 30-Oct-2009 | Milward |
| Glacken Brenda | 27 | 17 | 4 | 27-May-1995 | Ramsey |
| Gleason Pope Dorothy | 32 | 10 | 4 | 29-Jun-1998 | Schoppen-host |
| Gleich Dolores | 30 | 128 | 7 | 12-Apr-2000 | Spurlin |
| Glenn Letha | 29A | 50 | 5 | 5-Aug-2002 | Ramsey |
| Godber Austin | 33 | 59 | 3&4 | 10-Jan-2001 | Ramsey |
| Godfrey Ewina | 25 | 25 | 14 | 10-Apr-1999 | Ramsey |
| Goens Stella | 30 | 30 | 3 | 2-Feb-1999 | Ramsey |
| Goens Tina | 33 | 30 | 1 | 8-Nov-2008 | Spurlin |
| Goetz Rose | 33 | 1 | | 27-Mar-2006 | Sears |
| Goins B. Willie | 23 | 25 | 9 | 5-Apr-2000 | Spurlin |
| Goins Debra | 31 | 19 | 1 | 21-Dec-2006 | Spurlin |
| Goins Gene | 34 | 48 | 6 | 6-May-2005 | Ramsey |
| Goins P. J. | 30 | 95 | 4 | 24-Mar-2004 | Ramsey |
| Goins R. James | 34 | 57 | 4 | 24-Aug-2007 | Ramsey |
| Gomez Linda | 24 | 26 | 7 | 9-Jul-2008 | Kerr Bros |
| Gosney Lillie | 24 | 26 | 5 | 30-Sep-1998 | Kerr Bros |
| Graham Anita | 29A | 99 | 1 | 2-Jun-2007 | Best & West |
| Graham Charlie | 33 | 7 | 8 | 26-Jan-2004 | Ramsey |
| Graham Chester | 33 | 28 | 2 | 15-Mar-1997 | Ramsey |
| Graham Clarence | 33 | 35 | 6 | 24-Jan-2005 | Ramsey |
| Graham Clay | 25 | 38 | 9 | 7-Sep-2001 | Ramsey |
| Graham Dollie | 33 | 52 | 5 | 25-Apr-1998 | Stith |
| Graham Gordon | 30 | 100 | 2 | 7-Apr-2003 | Ramsey |
| Graham Hattie | 12 | 43 | 2 | 7-Aug-1996 | Ramsey |
| Graham James | 33 | 52 | 6 | 28-Dec-2001 | Stith |
| Graham Jennifer | 33 | 17 | 4 | 13-Dec-2001 | Ramsey |

| Name | Sec | Lot | Grave | Interment Date | Director |
|------|-----|-----|-------|---------------|----------|
| Graham Jewell | 22 | 18 | 7 | 22-Jun-1995 | Ramsey |
| Graham Mary | 29A | 58 | 3 | 30-Jul-2009 | Ramsey |
| Graham Oakley | 30 | 150 | 8 | 24-Apr-2000 | Ramsey |
| Graham R. James | 33 | 11 | 8 | 3-Nov-2006 | Ramsey |
| Graham Stella | 33 | 20 | 1 | 5-Feb-2009 | Spurlin |
| Graham Walter | 22 | 2 | 8 | 17-Nov-1999 | Ramsey |
| Graham William | 29A | 99 | 6 | 20-Aug-1996 | Ramsey |
| Grant Hattie | 20 | 61 | 12 | 11-Dec-2006 | Ramsey |
| Green Beverly | 16 | 53 | 3 | 7-Jan-1995 | Ramsey |
| Greer S. Patsy | 34 | 33 | 5 | 1-Feb-2007 | Spurlin |
| Gregory P. Ira | 29 | 27 | 10 | 31-May-2007 | Spurlin |
| Gregory Willard | 30 | 70 | 4 | 15-Oct-2009 | Spurlin |
| Grider Adeline | 33 | 48 | 3 | 14-Apr-1999 | Ramsey |
| Griggs William | 23 | 33 | 7 | 4-Apr-1998 | Ramsey |
| Grimes Elizabeth | 27 | 22 | 1 | 6-Jul-1998 | Ramsey |
| Grimes Fannie | 29A | 126 | 7 | 19-Apr-1997 | Ramsey |
| Grimes Kirby | 32 | 17 | 8 | 23-Mar-2006 | Ramsey |
| Grimes Lee Mary | 12 | 45 | 5 | 15-Feb-2001 | Spurlin |
| Grimes Minnie | 25 | 14 | 1 | 20-Nov-2007 | Spurlin |
| Grimes Paul | 27 | 34 | 4 | 29-Aug-2007 | Lusk |
| Grimes William | 34 | 27 | 4 | 24-Dec-2003 | Spurlin |
| Grow Charlene | 21 | 20 | 14 | 16-Jan-2004 | Ramsey |
| Grow Della | 4 | 26 | 14 | 2-Jul-2004 | Ramsey |
| Grow Elgan | 21 | 17 | 16 | 21-Nov-2005 | Ramsey |
| Grow Fannie | 19 | 5 | 16 | 20-Sep-1995 | Ramsey |
| Grow Robert | 30 | 63 | 2 | 25-Aug-1998 | Ramsey |
| Grubbs Arthur | 30 | 14 | 6 | 22-Jun-1995 | Carey |
| Grubbs Earl | 29A | 85 | 8 | 29-May-2003 | Ramsey |

| Name | Sec | Lot | Grave | Interment Date | Director |
|---|---|---|---|---|---|
| Grubbs Eugene | 18 | 48 | 3 | 5-Jul-2002 | Ramsey |
| Grubbs Herbert | 23 | 19 | 3 | 17-Dec-2009 | Spurlin |
| Grubbs John | 23 | 19 | 12 | 5-Jan-1996 | Ramsey |
| Grubbs Nannie | 30 | 14 | 5 | 9-Aug-2005 | Carey |
| Grubbs Roger | 29 | 17 | 7 | 7-Jun-1997 | Spurlin |
| Grubbs Stella | 29 | 17 | 6 | 21-May-2008 | Spurlin |
| Gulley Ann | 7 | 15 | 1 | 22-Sep-2001 | |
| Gutierrez Christian | 27 | 2 | 16 | 14-Feb-2006 | Ramsey |
| Guyn Robert | 24 | 33 | 8 | 5-Jan-1998 | Spurlin |
| Gwyn William | 8 | 1 | 12 | 1-Jul-2005 | Spurlin |
| Hale A. David | 30 | 151 | 4 | 26-Jan-2005 | |
| Hale Clarence | 30 | 82 | 6 | 12-Jun-2006 | Ramsey |
| Hale Coy | 30 | 151 | 6 | 28-Oct-2010 | Ramsey |
| Hall Billy | 30 | 172 | 4 | 20-Nov-2003 | Ramsey |
| Hall Bobby (Jr.) | 31 | 1 | 3 | 25-Mar-2006 | Spurlin |
| Hall Joseph | 30 | 171 | 1 | 28-Jan-2008 | Ramsey |
| Hall Laura | 29A | 49 | 5 | 17-Jun-1997 | Ramsey |
| Hall Nola | 30 | 17 | 7 | 5-Oct-2007 | Ramsey |
| Hall Randal David | 33 | 53 | 1 | 2-Apr-1999 | Ramsey |
| Hall Ruby | 27 | 7 | 6 | 21-Nov-1996 | Ramsey |
| Hamilton Charles | 16 | 2 | 6 | 2-Dec-1996 | Ramsey |
| Hamilton Gertie | 18 | 2 | 1 | 7-Apr-2000 | Ramsey |
| Hamilton Hazel | 18 | 2 | 15 | 21-Jan-2002 | Ramsey |
| Hamilton L. James | 31 | 11 | 4 | 5-Sep-2009 | Spurlin |
| Hamm Everett | 30 | 51 | 4 | 9-Jan-1995 | Harrod Bros |
| Hammonds Charles | 16 | 29 | 11 | 7-Dec-2005 | Ramsey |
| Hammonds Leola | 23 | 4 | 3 | 8-Apr-1995 | Ramsey |
| Hammonds Margaret | 16 | 29 | 10 | 9-Feb-1999 | Ramsey |

| Name | Sec | Lot | Grave | Interment Date | Director |
|---|---|---|---|---|---|
| Hammonds W. Joe | 16 | 29 | 2 | 1-Nov-2008 | |
| Hammons Herbert | 29 | 30 | 14 | 25-Mar-1999 | Ramsey |
| Handy Lana | 33 | 41 | 1 | 13-Aug-2007 | Barkes |
| Handy R. Randell | 33 | 41 | 2 | 3-Jan-1995 | Barkes |
| Harden Brian | 16 | 18 | 5 | 19-Jun-1999 | Ramsey |
| Harden William | 33 | 58 | 8 | 21-Mar-2005 | Ramsey |
| Hardwick Audrey | 30 | 70 | 1 | 23-Dec-1998 | Ramsey |
| Hardwick Clayton | 23 | 27 | 8 | 3-Apr-1995 | Ramsey |
| Hardwick Doris | 29A | 125 | 3 | 25-Nov-2003 | Ramsey |
| Hardwick Virgil | 30 | 70 | 2 | 14-Jul-1998 | Ramsey |
| Hardwick Willie | 34 | 3 | 8 | 12-Sep-2006 | Ramsey |
| Harmon Frances | 32 | 9 | 5 | 12-May-2009 | Spurlin |
| Harness James | 30 | 135 | 2 | 8-Jun-2000 | McNight |
| Harris Elizabeth | 24 | 9 | 4 | 28-Dec-2001 | Beam Fender |
| Harris Hamilton | 20 | 7 | 5 | 15-Feb-1995 | Milward |
| Harris S. Edith | 29A | 87 | 1 | 22-Apr-2004 | Ramsey |
| Harrison Carl | 30 | 127 | 8 | 27-Aug-2001 | Ramsey |
| Harrison Richard | 21 | 4 | 3 | 26-Jun-2007 | Combs |
| Harrison Zada | 21 | 4 | 1 | 22-Feb-2010 | Combs |
| Haselden Laverne | 25 | 7 | 2 | 13-Jun-1998 | |
| Hatchell Harold | 26 | 14 | 15 | 19-Apr-2002 | Ramsey |
| Hatfield Jewell | 30 | 161 | 1 | 1-Aug-2007 | Ramsey |
| Hatfiled Geneva | 30 | 27 | 3 | 7-Jul-2003 | Spurlin |
| Hatfiled J. A. | 23 | 39 | 13 | 5-Nov-2004 | Alexander |
| Hawkins Diana | 11 | 8 | 9 | 21-Feb-2004 | |
| Hawkins Frank | 30 | 37 | 6 | 8-Feb-1997 | Spurlin |
| Hayner Kevin | 34 | 40 | 4 | 8-Sep-2003 | Spurlin |

| Name | Sec | Lot | Grave | Interment Date | Director |
|------|-----|-----|-------|----------------|----------|
| Hays Shelagh | 24 | 20 | 7 | 21-Jun-1997 | |
| Hays William | 24 | 20 | 8 | 22-Jul-2000 | |
| Heare Katherine | 30 | 95 | 1 | 31-Jul-1999 | Ramsey |
| Hearn O. Joseph | 7 | 8 | 9 | 29-Mar-2004 | Ramsey |
| Heipley B. Geneva | 12 | 24 | 12 | 30-Jul-2009 | Ramsey |
| Helton Alex (Jr.) | 34 | 27 | 2 | 21-Apr-2001 | Spurlin |
| Helton Bell Anna | 20 | 52 | 10 | 7-Aug-1999 | Williams |
| Helton Forest | 30 | 12 | 4 | 8-Apr-1995 | McNight |
| Helton Justin | 33 | 16 | 4 | 6-Aug-2004 | Ramsey |
| Helton Mildred | 34 | 27 | 1 | 21-Apr-2006 | Ramsey |
| Henderson Cecil | 16 | 1 | 10 | 7-Apr-2009 | Ramsey |
| Henderson Etta | 16 | 1 | 9 | 12-Mar-1997 | Ramsey |
| Hendren Vera | 26 | 20 | 6 | 22-Dec-1997 | Oldman |
| Hendrickson Ada | 17 | 19 | 10 | 17-Jul-2002 | Ramsey |
| Hendrickson William | 29 | 28 | 14 | 21-Nov-1995 | Ramsey |
| Henry Corrina | 32 | 19 | 4 | 25-Jan-2003 | Ramsey |
| Henry E. James | 19 | 6 | 2 | 19-May-2008 | Ramsey |
| Henry Louise | 17 | 18 | 11 | 22-Jan-2010 | Ramsey |
| Henry Mattie | 14 | 5 | 2 | 12-Sep-1996 | Ramsey |
| Henry T. Robert | 29 | 6 | 10 | 5-Dec-2009 | Spurlin |
| Herring Delsie | 30 | 56 | 1 | 28-Aug-1997 | Ramsey |
| Hest Trevor | 21 | 13 | 16 | 28-Nov-1997 | Spurlin |
| Hester Evelyn | 23 | 29 | 15 | 20-Nov-2002 | Spurlin |
| Hester Russell | 23 | 24 | 16 | 30-Dec-2004 | Spurlin |
| Hester Ryan Noah | 21 | 13 | 16 | 3-Jul-1998 | Spurlin |
| Hester Scott | 24 | 28 | 9 | 5-Nov-2009 | Ramsey |
| Hicks Elizabeth | 7 | 18 | 16 | 14-Oct-2000 | Common-wealth |

| Name | Sec | Lot | Grave | Interment Date | Director |
|---|---|---|---|---|---|
| Hicks Oma | 32 | 2 | 5 | 24-Apr-2000 | Ramsey |
| Hinderer Desirer | 34 | 52 | 5 | 14-May-2008 | Preston Pruitt |
| Hinds Albert | 31 | 13 | 3 | 23-May-2007 | Ramsey |
| Hockney Raymond | 30 | 56 | 8 | 3-Jul-2010 | Ramsey |
| Holtzclaw Dorothy | 5 | 41 | 16 | 7-Mar-2003 | Ramsey |
| Holtzclaw Gladys | 25 | 7 | 10 | 7-Jan-2004 | Preston Pruitt |
| Holtzclaw Ora | 23 | 20 | 1 | 26-Oct-2001 | Spurlin |
| Holtzclaw Rex | 23 | 24 | 9 | 23-Sep-2008 | Spurlin |
| Hopkins Fannie | 33 | 33 | 1 | 23-Nov-1998 | Ramsey |
| Hopkins Raymond | 33 | 33 | 2 | 25-Mar-1995 | Ramsey |
| Hopkins Rosie | 15 | | 9 | 14-Nov-1997 | Ramsey |
| Hornsby Orie | 21 | 15 | 1 | 10-Jul-1995 | Ramsey |
| Horsman Walter | 29A | 132 | 2 | 28-Jul-1997 | Ramsey |
| Horton Juanita | 33 | 6 | 7 | 27-Feb-1995 | Ramsey |
| Horseman Grace | 29A | 132 | 1 | 13-Jun-2001 | Ramsey |
| House Sallie | 16 | 18 | 12 | 16-Dec-1998 | Ramsey |
| Houston Terri | 26 | 7 | 1 | 6-Feb-2001 | Lange |
| Howard Barbara | 33 | 11 | 2 | 3-Oct-2003 | Spurlin |
| Howard Beulah | 24 | 2 | 2 | 12-Apr-2008 | Combs |
| Howard Buford | 32 | 13 | 6 | 26-Oct-2007 | Spurlin |
| Howard Carl | 29 | 12 | 14 | 5-May-1998 | Ramsey |
| Howard D. James | 34 | 17 | 2 | 15-Feb-2008 | Ramsey |
| Howard Larry | 34 | 50 | 3 | 18-Aug-2009 | Spurlin |
| Howard Lydia | 29 | 34 | 2 | 5-Apr-1996 | Ramsey |
| Howard Orville | 33 | 56 | 6 | 17-Jul-2001 | Ramsey |
| Howard Patricia | 20 | 52 | 3 | 1-Feb-2007 | Ramsey |

| Name | Sec | Lot | Grave | Interment Date | Director |
|---|---|---|---|---|---|
| Howard Sarah | 33 | 10 | 4 | 2-Oct-2007 | Spurlin |
| Howard Simpson Frances | 30 | 27 | 5 | 18-Mar-2000 | Spurlin |
| Hubbard R. Edward | 18 | 9 | 14 | 5-Mar-1998 | Dowell & Martin |
| Hudson Martha | 29A | 118 | 3 | 15-Jul-2002 | Ramsey |
| Hudson Mary | 16 | 54 | 12 | 12-Feb-1998 | Ramsey |
| Huffman C. Mary | 28 | 7 | 9 | 30-Sep-2008 | Clark |
| Huffman Curry | 20 | 39 | 13 | 1-Sep-1997 | Ramsey |
| Huffman Gertrude | 29 | 19 | 2 | 6-Oct-2009 | Ramsey |
| Huffman Harlan | 29 | 19 | 11 | 19-Dec-1997 | Ramsey |
| Huffman Harold | 27 | 10 | 15 | 19-Jan-2005 | Stith |
| Huffman Ida | 11 | 10 | 1 | 15-Jun-2005 | Oldman |
| Huffman Joe | 33 | 18 | 4 | 18-Jan-2006 | Ramsey |
| Huffman June | 12 | 17 | 1 | 25-Aug-1999 | Spurlin |
| Huffman K. James (Jr.) | 7 | 20 | 1 | 21-Oct-2005 | |
| Huffman L. Dora | 20 | 47 | 3 | 25-Feb-1999 | Ramsey |
| Huffman Leola | 27 | 10 | 14 | 3-Feb-2007 | Spurlin |
| Huffman Raymond | 20 | 38 | 8 | 5-Sep-1998 | Ramsey |
| Huffman Robert | 28 | 7 | 10 | 12-Aug-2008 | Clark |
| Huffman Sharron | 21 | 32 | 8 | 17-Oct-2008 | Spurlin |
| Huffman Stella | 29 | 19 | 14 | 29-Nov-2001 | Ramsey |
| Huffman William | 27 | 10 | 11 | 15-Aug-2003 | Spurlin |
| Hughe D. A. | 20 | 43 | 12 | 27-Jan-2001 | Ramsey |
| Hughes Margaret | 30 | 43 | 10 | 28-Apr-2010 | Ramsey |
| Huglin Morgorie | 18 | 10 | 1 | 27-Mar-1998 | |
| Hulett Calvin (Jr.) | 23 | 2 | 4 | 25-Jun-2008 | Ramsey |
| Hulett Ralph | 23 | 2 | 6 | 14-Feb-2005 | Ramsey |

| Name | Sec | Lot | Grave | Interment Date | Director |
|------|-----|-----|-------|----------------|----------|
| Hulett Rebecca | 23 | 5 | 8 | 24-May-1995 | Ramsey |
| Hume Burnette | 27 | 15 | 12 | 12-Dec-2000 | Spurlin |
| Hume Charlie | 20 | 53 | 6 | 29-Jan-1999 | Ramsey |
| Hume Donald James | 32 | 33 | 4 | 28-Dec-2001 | Spurlin |
| Hume Lois | 20 | 53 | 5 | 7-Nov-2001 | Ramsey |
| Hume Travis | 33 | 29 | 6 | 10-Dec-2009 | Spurlin |
| Hume Wilma | 33 | 29 | 5 | 10-Dec-2009 | Spurlin |
| Humphrey Allie | 34 | 38 | 1 | 3-Apr-2010 | Spurlin |
| Humphrey E. James | 30 | 31 | 8 | 5-Jun-2002 | Ramsey |
| Humphrey Eva | 30 | 141 | 5 | 12-Oct-2001 | Ramsey |
| Humphrey Felix | 29 | 31 | 16 | 4-Dec-2000 | Ramsey |
| Humphrey Frances Minnie | 24 | 8 | 16 | 28-Jan-2002 | Ramsey |
| Humphrey Gertrude | 24 | 8 | 4 | 19-Feb-1999 | Ramsey |
| Humphrey Jess | 29 | 31 | 8 | 13-Mar-1998 | Spurlin |
| Humphrey Nola | 18 | 11 | 16 | 21-Nov-2000 | Ramsey |
| Hunter A. Dolly | 4 | 26 | 14 | 2-Jul-2004 | Ramsey |
| Hurt Allene | 29A | 48 | 1 | 10-Jun-1999 | Ramsey |
| Hurt Elizabeth | 29A | 47 | 3 | 26-Nov-2001 | Spurlin |
| Hurt Geneva | 26 | 14 | 4 | 12-May-2006 | Ramsey |
| Hurt Henry (Jr.) | 29A | 48 | 2 | 7-Feb-2003 | Ramsey |
| Hurt Ralph | 26 | 14 | 5 | 11-Nov-2006 | Spurlin |
| Hurt Teater Kirby | 29 | 35 | 11 | 21-Jan-1995 | Ramsey |
| Hurt Thomas | 34 | 23 | 8 | 27-Aug-2008 | Ramsey |
| Irvin Doris | 11 | 5 | 2 | 6-Jul-2007 | Ramsey |
| Irvin Kenneth | 30 | 156 | 8 | 5-Nov-2007 | Ramsey |
| Irvine Maudie | 20 | 41 | 21 | 23-Apr-2002 | Ramsey |
| Isaacs Bowen | 30 | 15 | 6 | 3-Mar-1995 | Ramsey |

| Name | Sec | Lot | Grave | Interment Date | Director |
|---|---|---|---|---|---|
| Isaacs Lessie | 33 | 58 | 4 | 25-Jun-2007 | Ramsey |
| Isaacs Marie | 24 | 21 | 1 | 28-Dec-2004 | Spurlin |
| Isaacs P.O. | 24 | 21 | 8 | 28-Jun-2007 | Spurlin |
| Ison Earl | 24 | 7 | 6 | 6-Apr-2004 | Best & West |
| Ison Virgil | 24 | 7 | 5 | 10-Jul-1995 | Best & West |
| Jacobson Maude | 29A | 59 | 3 | 7-Mar-2001 | Spurlin |
| Jenkins Bessie | 21 | 30 | 3 | 7-Jan-1999 | Ramsey |
| Jenkins Talbot | 29 | 28 | 3 | 17-Jan-1995 | Ramsey |
| Jennings Charles | 5 | 38 | WW | 3-Jun-2004 | Ramsey |
| Jennings Sue | 3 | 29 | 7 | 22-Jul-1997 | Ramsey |
| Johnica J. A. | 33 | 55 | 3 | 28-Jul-1998 | Ramsey |
| Johns James | 29A | 93 | 1 | 19-Jul-1999 | Coots |
| Johnson Alma | 32 | 4 | 5 | 12-Apr-2003 | Ramsey |
| Johnson Blake Austin | 19 | 19 | 14 | 9-Jan-1999 | Spurlin |
| Johnson C. Jo. Betty | 9 | 6 | 12 | 28-Mar-2006 | Stith |
| Johnson Danny | 14 | 16 | 14 | 18-Oct-2006 | Ramsey |
| Johnson James | 14 | 16 | 16 | 26-Jul-2007 | Ramsey |
| Johnson Jean | 22 | 13 | 2 | 18-Jun-2005 | Ramsey |
| Johnson Shirley | 33 | 26 | 8 | 1-Jul-2004 | Ramsey |
| Johnson Virginia | 2 | 17 | 16 | 15-Feb-2000 | Preston Pruitt |
| Johnston Rodney | 34 | 8 | 6 | 7-Jul-2008 | Spurlin |
| Jones B. J. | 16 | 55 | 5 | 9-Jan-2006 | Ramsey |
| Jones Clara | 26 | 4 | 14 | 27-Oct-2008 | Ramsey |
| Jones Marilyn | 29A | 89 | 5 | 6-Sep-2008 | Heady & Hardy |
| Jones Richard | 30 | 59 | 4 | 11-Dec-1995 | Ramsey |
| Joseph Georgia | 30 | 159 | 8 | 7-Apr-2006 | Ramsey |
| Karnes Hazel | 26 | 12 | 14 | 17-Jun-2002 | Spurlin |

| Name | Sec | Lot | Grave | Interment Date | Director |
|---|---|---|---|---|---|
| Karnes James | 26 | 12 | 15 | 14-Jun-1995 | Ramsey |
| Keeling Dorothy | 33 | 49 | 3 | 12-Dec-1998 | Spurlin |
| Keeling William | 33 | 49 | 4 | 13-May-2005 | Spurlin |
| Kelly Scott Chester | 25 | 21 | 6 | 25-Mar-2002 | Ramsey |
| Kern Ruth | 5 | 8 | 11 | 3-Sep-2005 | Ramsey |
| Kersey Nellie | 8 | 15 | 1 | 15-Feb-2001 | Ramsey |
| Kidd Emma | 23 | 28 | 1 | 2-Aug-2004 | Somerset |
| Kimble Hazel | 2 | 17 | 1 | 26-Jun-2000 | |
| King A. William | 34 | 55 | 2 | 16-Nov-2009 | Stith |
| King Marie | 20 | 24 | 9 | 4-May-1996 | Ramsey |
| King Mayme | 27 | 5 | 5 | 14-Apr-2000 | Spurlin |
| King Nathan | 20 | 24 | 10 | 11-Sep-2008 | Ramsey |
| King Thomas | 33 | 47 | 8 | 11-Feb-1998 | Ramsey |
| Kirby Leonard | 32 | 24 | 2 | 28-Aug-2000 | Ramsey |
| Kurtz Anna | 25 | 29 | 1 | 10-May-1995 | Ramsey |
| Kurtz Harold | 36 | 1 | 8 | 23-Jul-2010 | Ramsey |
| Kurtz Roberta | 29A | 56 | 5 | 20-Oct-2010 | Ramsey |
| Lake Addie | 18 | 31 | 10 | 7-Jun-2007 | Kerr Bros |
| Lamb Alma | 30 | 102 | 7 | 9-Sep-1999 | Spurlin |
| Lamb Annie | 20 | 10 | 7 | 8-Jul-1998 | Spurlin |
| Lamb George | 30 | 103 | 6 | 30-Nov-1996 | Ramsey |
| Lamb Julian | 12 | 45 | 3 | 22-Oct-2008 | Spurlin |
| Lamb Mary | 30 | 32 | 1 | 23-Jun-1995 | Ramsey |
| Lamb Virgil | 30 | 32 | 2 | 1-Jul-2000 | Spurlin |
| Lambert Ruth | 16 | 47 | 10 | 7-Jan-2000 | Ramsey |
| Lancaster James | 18 | 25 | 2 | 21-Jan-2005 | Spurlin |
| Land Billy | 34 | 13 | 4 | 31-Mar-2008 | Ramsey |
| Land K. Mary | 25 | 2 | 10 | 15-Feb-2010 | Ramsey |

| Name | Sec | Lot | Grave | Interment Date | Director |
|---|---|---|---|---|---|
| Lane Cecil | 20 | 40 | 1A | 3-Jan-1998 | Ramsey |
| Lane David | 33 | 62 | 2 | 26-Oct-2000 | Ramsey |
| Lane Donald | 16 | 40 | 4 | 24-Oct-2001 | Ramsey |
| Lane E. Nora | 26 | 17 | 6 | 13-Apr-2001 | Spurlin |
| Lane Geneva | 30 | 48 | 5 | 26-Apr-2000 | Ramsey |
| Lane George | 33 | 62 | 4 | 22-Apr-2004 | Spurlin |
| Lane Georgia | 33 | 29 | 3 | 6-Mar-2003 | Spurlin |
| Lane Minnie | 16 | 40 | 3 | 17-Mar-2004 | Ramsey |
| Lane Ruby | 34 | 1 | 8 | 22-Jun-2005 | Spurlin |
| Lane Sallie | 23 | 31 | 11 | 7-Jul-1999 | Ramsey |
| Lane Vernon | 34 | 2 | 6 | 9-Feb-2002 | Spurlin |
| Lane Wilbur | 34 | 2 | 7 | 5-Jun-2003 | Spurlin |
| Lanter John | 33 | 43 | 4 | 8-Feb-1999 | Combs |
| LaPierre Elsie | 28 | 18 | 16 | 8-Nov-1999 | Kerr Bros |
| Lauson A. Margaret | 7 | 2 | 3 | 17-Apr-2010 | |
| Lawson Earl | 30 | 51 | 2 | 6-Jan-1998 | Fox |
| Lawson Lucille | 25 | 32 | 2 | 3-Apr-1996 | Ramsey |
| Lay Gracie | 30 | 61 | 7 | 22-Feb-1997 | Ramsey |
| Lay Vernon | 31 | 19 | 6 | 22-May-2004 | Spurlin |
| Lay Virginia | 30 | 178 | 3 | 8-Dec-2004 | Stith |
| Layton Cecil | 34 | 47 | 2 | 3-Sep-2007 | Ramsey |
| Layton Della | 30 | 113 | 3 | 17-May-2000 | Ramsey |
| Layton Emma | 8 | 7 | 11 | 11-Nov-2003 | Ramsey |
| Layton Geneva | 2 | 26 | 6 | 12-Mar-1996 | Ramsey |
| Layton George | 2 | 26 | 7 | 10-Jul-1999 | Ramsey |
| Layton Geraldine | 21 | 21 | 2 | 20-Dec-1999 | Ramsey |
| Layton John | 30 | 113 | 4 | 3-Feb-1996 | Ramsey |
| Layton Lewis | 18 | 33 | 1A | 16-Feb-2007 | Ramsey |

| Name | Sec | Lot | Grave | Interment Date | Director |
|---|---|---|---|---|---|
| Layton Lucille | 2 | 17 | 11 | 24-Nov-1998 | Parrot & Ramsey |
| Layton Ray Inez | 25 | 38 | 4 | 25-Nov-1997 | Duell Clark |
| Layton Ruby | 18 | 35 | 2 | 15-Mar-1999 | Ramsey |
| Layton Steve | 22 | 12 | 4 | 17-Jun-2000 | Ramsey |
| Layton William | 18 | 35 | 10 | 7-Feb-2002 | Ramsey |
| League John | 33 | 63 | 1 | 8-Dec-2004 | Ramsey |
| Leaque Bonnie | 33 | 34 | 1 | 30-Apr-1997 | Ramsey |
| Lear Dorothy | 33 | 52 | 1 | 22-Mar-1999 | Ramsey |
| Lear Verna | 12 | 17 | 2 | 12-Dec-1995 | Ramsey |
| Leavell Ben | 4 | 27 | 16 | 16-Oct-1996 | Ramsey |
| Leavelle Bob | 4 | 27 | 15 | 20-Jan-2001 | Ramsey |
| LeBrun Mathew | 33 | 43 | 2 | 15-Aug-1997 | Spurlin |
| Ledford Coy | 29A | 39 | 6 | 6-Nov-1997 | McNight |
| Ledford Evelyn | 29 | 23 | 11 | 18-Feb-2006 | Pearson |
| Ledford Mauhee | 33 | 53 | 5 | 29-Jan-2000 | Ramsey |
| Lee Clyde | 24 | 29 | 3 | 20-Apr-2005 | Kerr Bros |
| Lee Gilbert | 11 | 40 | 10 | 11-Apr-1998 | Ramsey |
| Lee Homer | 33 | 54 | 6 | 7-Apr-2003 | Spurlin |
| Lee Loriene | 33 | 59 | 5 | 10-Jan-2001 | Spurlin |
| Lee U. Robert | 17 | 10 | * | 19-Aug-2006 | Spurlin |
| Leet Jewell | 26 | 8 | 7 | 31-Aug-2002 | Best & West |
| Lehrschall Allene | 30 | 13 | 3&4 | 17-Sep-1999 | Preston Pruitt |
| Lemay Durward | 20 | 49 | 5&6 | 9-Jul-2002 | |
| Lemay Nancy | 27 | 3 | 11 | 10-Mar-2008 | Stith |
| Lester Wilmot Mattie | 16 | 16 | 11 | 28-Dec-1999 | Stith |
| Lewis Hadgie | 34 | 17 | 3 | 30-Dec-2002 | Spurlin |

* Cremains buried at the back of Grave # 15

| Name | Sec | Lot | Grave | Interment Date | Director |
|------|-----|-----|-------|----------------|----------|
| Lewis M. Anna | 28 | 4 | 15 | 20-Jun-2005 | Tucker |
| Lewis Morgan | 34 | 17 | 4 | 19-May-2003 | Spurlin |
| Libby Jean Clara | 5 | 13 | 15 | 4-Jun-1999 | Spurlin |
| Lockard Lloyd | 34 | 62 | 3 | 16-Feb-2006 | Spurlin |
| Locker Chester | 22 | 17 | 11 | 16-May-2006 | Ramsey |
| Locker Hazel | 22 | 17 | 10 | 31-Dec-2003 | Ramsey |
| Logan Bill | 23 | 39 | 7 | 17-Nov-1997 | Ramsey |
| Logan Dwight | 20 | 42 | 11 | 5-Oct-1998 | Ramsey |
| Logan Pearl | 21 | 3 | 11 | 21-Feb-1998 | Ramsey |
| Logan Roberta | 23 | 39 | 6 | 13-Sep-1999 | Ramsey |
| Lombardo Peters Helen | 17 | 5 | 8 | 13-Jun-1999 | |
| Long Ada | 30 | 27 | 4 | 23-Sep-2004 | Spurlin |
| Long Allie | 24 | 17 | 10 | 30-Jun-2003 | Ramsey |
| Long Bill | 30 | 107 | 4 | 5-Sep-1998 | Ramsey |
| Long C. Q. | 34 | 28 | 8 | 6-Dec-2005 | Ramsey |
| Long Christine | 33 | 56 | 1 | 27-Jul-2001 | Ramsey |
| Long Ethel | 34 | 28 | 7 | 9-Sep-2002 | Ramsey |
| Long Eugene | 9 | 28 | 11 | 24-Apr-2002 | Spurlin |
| Long Frances | 29A | 105 | 5 | 20-Jul-2000 | Spurlin |
| Long Hazel | 33 | 62 | 5 | 20-Nov-2004 | Spurlin |
| Long James | 34 | 32 | 6 | 20-Jan-2003 | Ramsey |
| Long Johnny | 33 | 56 | 2 | 7-Feb-2000 | Ramsey |
| Long M. Anna | 25 | 33 | 9 | 29-May-2001 | Ramsey |
| Long Woodrow | 16 | 44 | 13 | 27-Oct-2010 | Ramsey |
| Lucas B. Elmer | 20 | 61 | 16 | 24-Jul-2000 | Ramsey |
| Lunsford John | 22 | 1 | 16 | 25-May-2007 | Stith |
| Lynch Viola | 21 | 31 | 10 | 5-Feb-2001 | Spurlin |

| Name | Sec | Lot | Grave | Interment Date | Director |
|---|---|---|---|---|---|
| Lynn B. J. | 33 | 16 | 2 | 10-May-1996 | Ramsey |
| Lyons Vivian | 20 | 62 | | 21-Oct-2005 | Ramsey |
| MacWitley Jack | 15 | | | 20-Mar-1998 | |
| Major Dallas | 33 | 52 | 3 | 11-May-1998 | Ramsey |
| Malear Chester | 23 | 32 | 1 | 11-Jan-2003 | Ramsey |
| Malear Leo | 23 | 32 | 12 | 21-Jul-2004 | Ramsey |
| Malear Lida | 23 | 32 | 11 | 3-Jan-2006 | Ramsey |
| Marcum Brian | 33 | 73 | 3 | 23-Nov-2009 | Spurlin |
| Marpin Calvin | 28 | 12 | | 13-Oct-2007 | |
| Marsee Edd | 20 | 34 | 13 | 15-Nov-1995 | Ramsey |
| Marsee Ida | 32 | 4 | 7 | 15-Dec-1995 | Ramsey |
| Marsee Stanley | 32 | 4 | 8 | 21-Jul-1995 | Ramsey |
| Marsee W. John | 29S | 67 | 6 | 6-Sep-2008 | Ramsey |
| Martin Dorothy | 29A | 58 | 1 | 24-Oct-2009 | Stith |
| Masser Ray | 29A | 83 | 5 | 24-Sep-2007 | Ramsey |
| Masters Charles | 24 | 6 | 15 | 28-Mar-2000 | Ramsey |
| Masters Dorothy | 24 | 6 | 14 | 7-Mar-2000 | Ramsey |
| Mathews Folger Mary | 7 | 30 | 2 | 10-Apr-2001 | Milward |
| Mathews James | 33 | 55 | 6 | 30-Aug-2004 | Ramsey |
| Mathews Mary | 33 | 53 | 4 | 24-Jan-2000 | Ramsey |
| Mathis Elizabeth | 29A | 139 | 3 | 24-Mar-1995 | Ramsey |
| Matlock Permrelia | 27 | 21 | 9 | 27-Jun-1998 | Ramsey |
| Maupin Doris | 22 | 11 | 7 | 7-Jan-2010 | Ramsey |
| Maupin Elby | 30 | 45 | 8 | 5-Oct-1999 | Ramsey |
| Maupin Frances | 22 | 11 | 4 | 28-Sep-2010 | Ramsey |
| Maupin John | 32 | 17 | 4 | 6-Apr-2002 | Ramsey |
| Maupin June | 30 | 144 | 7 | 5-Feb-2010 | Ramsey |
| Maupin Robert | 22 | 11 | 3 | 21-Aug-1995 | Ramsey |

| Name | Sec | Lot | Grave | Interment Date | Director |
|---|---|---|---|---|---|
| May (Hawl) Beatrice | 20 | 40 | 14 | 5-Aug-1995 | Radall |
| May Garnett | 25 | 33 | 5 | 17-Jul-1998 | Ramsey |
| May Hazel | 27 | 29 | 12 | 2-Feb-1996 | Best & West |
| May Hope | 30 | 39 | 7 | 6-Jan-2005 | Spurlin |
| May Mabel | 16 | 22 | 16 | 15-Jul-1999 | Ramsey |
| May Paul | 30 | 46 | 5 | 30-May-1998 | Ramsey |
| May Reba | 33 | 8 | 3 | 6-May-2005 | Spurlin |
| May Steve | 32 | 6 | 7 | 12-Aug-2003 | Ramsey |
| Mayfield Charlie | 3 | 31 | 16 | 8-Feb-1995 | Ramsey |
| Mayfield Gay | 29A | 110 | 7 | 4-Aug-1998 | Ramsey |
| Mayfield Wilmot | 29A | 110 | 5 | 12-Dec-2005 | Ramsey |
| McCain Delores | 23 | 25 | 11 | 2-Jan-2002 | Spurlin |
| McCarty Ray Maggie | 11 | 20 | 7 | 10-Nov-2010 | Morgan & Nag (Indiana) |
| McClure Eran | 34 | 19 | 5 | 7-May-2005 | Ramsey |
| McCoy Hilda | 34 | 3 | 55 | 8-Mar-2008 | Spurlin |
| McCoy Raymond | 34 | 3 | 6 | 28-Dec-2004 | Spurlin |
| McCulley Bruce | 23 | 26 | 6 | 9-Jul-1998 | Ramsey |
| McCulley Effie | 23 | 41 | 11 | 11-May-1998 | Swaren |
| McCulley Opal | 30 | 16 | 3 | 8-Feb-2008 | Ramsey |
| McCully Billy | 33 | 45 | 5 | 30-Aug-1995 | Ramsey |
| McCully Oris | 30 | 12 | 6 | 25-Apr-1998 | Ramsey |
| McDowell Louise Mary | 5 | 19 | 9 | 14-May-1997 | Milward |
| McGlone Curtis | 33 | 53 | 8 | 11-Jan-2000 | Spurlin |
| McIlovy Ruby | 29A | 115 | 3 | 14-Aug-1999 | Ramsey |
| McKee Stella | 34 | 43 | 1 | 21-Jul-2008 | Ramsey |
| McKee Winnie | 28 | 3 | 1 | 25-Apr-2001 | Ramsey |

| Name | Sec | Lot | Grave | Interment Date | Director |
|------|-----|-----|-------|----------------|----------|
| McKenzie Beulah | 23 | 24 | 3 | 11-Jul-1995 | Ramsey |
| McKinney Florence | 29A | 90 | 3 | 29-Apr-1996 | McNight |
| McKinney Maurice | 29A | 90 | 4 | 8-Jan-1996 | McNight |
| McMurray Clark | 29A | 94 | 4 | 12-Apr-2002 | Ramsey |
| McNees Annie | 14 | 2 | 1 | 15-May-1995 | Ramsey |
| McQueary Anna | 27 | 26 | 14 | 18-Aug-2003 | Ramsey |
| McQueary Ardella | 30 | 41 | 7 | 6-Sep-2007 | Ramsey |
| McQueary Eliza | 23 | 1 | 15 | 12-May-1997 | Ramsey |
| McQueary Louis | 20 | 49 | 8 | 11-Sep-2003 | Spurlin |
| McQueary Robert (Jr.) | 30 | 41 | 4 | 23-Feb-2009 | Spurlin |
| McQuery Colman | 30 | 34 | 6 | 9-Jun-1997 | Ramsey |
| McWhorter M. Saundra | 30 | 46 | 8 | 8-Mar-2010 | Ramsey |
| Meadors Emory | 18 | 25 | 13 | 9-Sep-1997 | Ramsey |
| Meadows Elsie | 26 | 23 | 3 | 20-Jan-2001 | Ramsey |
| Meadows Geneva Georgia | 26 | 23 | 10 | 20-Oct-1998 | |
| Meadows Kelly | 30 | 104 | 3 | 8-Jul-2002 | Ramsey |
| Meadows Sallie | 18 | 25 | 12 | 25-May-2000 | Ramsey |
| Meadows William | 30 | 104 | 6 | 1-Jan-2008 | Ramsey |
| Medaries Helen | 18 | 15 | 5 | 13-Feb-2000 | |
| Meordors C. W. | 18 | 25 | 11 | 13-Dec-1996 | Ramsey |
| Mercer Bobby | 7 | 44 | 7 | 16-Aug-2004 | Spurlin |
| Merida Agnes | 11 | 4 | 7 | 16-Jan-1998 | Ramsey |
| Merida Clyde Sr. | 23 | 10 | 3 | 13-Aug-1996 | Ramsey |
| Merida Shirley | 21 | 11 | 14 | 8-Nov-1997 | Spurlin |
| Mershon Earl | 30 | 158 | 6 | 16-Jun-2010 | Ramsey |
| Metcalf Arnett | 33 | 41 | 6 | 23-Dec-1995 | Ramsey |

| Name | Sec | Lot | Grave | Interment Date | Director |
|---|---|---|---|---|---|
| Metcalfe Michelle | 34 | 50 | 8 | 24-May-2008 | Spurlin |
| Meyer Marie | 33 | 27 | 1 | 25-May-1996 | |
| Meyers P. Robert | 22 | 8 | 16 | 5-Dec-2005 | Young |
| Middleton Nancy | 33 | 28 | 5 | 24-Mar-1998 | Ramsey |
| Miller B. Thomas | 30 | 121 | 2 | 13-Aug-2007 | Spurlin |
| Miller B. Willie | 16 | 51 | 5 | 27-Oct-2004 | Spurlin |
| Miller Bobby | 33 | 6 | 1 | 5-May-2009 | Ramsey |
| Miller Elizabeth Mary | 33 | 5 | 4 | 25-Jun-1996 | Ramsey |
| Miller Janie | 24 | 28 | 6 | 6-Dec-2008 | Ramsey |
| Miller Lillian | 29A | 137 | 1 | 26-Jan-2006 | Spurlin |
| Miller Mason | 29A | 77 | 2 | 25-Aug-1998 | Spurlin |
| Miller Nelson | 33 | 32 | 4 | 24-Nov-1995 | Ramsey |
| Miller Ora Lee | 33 | 32 | 3 | 3-Feb-1995 | Ramsey |
| Miller Samuel B. | 30 | 121 | 4 | 22-Nov-1996 | Spurlin |
| Miller T. Mary | 30 | 75 | 7 | 10-Jul-2002 | Ramsey |
| Miller Walter (Jr.) | 27 | 2 | 2 | 10-Jun-2006 | Prewitt |
| Moberley Robert | 30 | 110 | 2 | 31-May-1996 | Combs |
| Moberly David | 33 | 65 | 2 | 4-May-2005 | Spurlin |
| Moberly Evelyn | 30 | 9 | 5 | 24-May-1999 | Ramsey |
| Moberly Lloyd | 30 | 106 | 8 | 22-Dec-2010 | Spurlin |
| Moberly P. Owen | 34 | 29 | 5 | 15-Nov-2002 | Hagen & Cundiff |
| Moberly Pauline | 34 | 29 | 7 | 20-Jan-2010 | Best & West |
| Moberly S. Jimmy | 34 | 45 | 6 | 12-Apr-2008 | Spurlin |
| Moberly Stella | 28 | 13 | 3 | 6-May-2002 | Spurlin |
| Moberly Verlinda | 30 | 158 | 7 | 24-Dec-2009 | Spurlin |
| Moberly William | 30 | 9 | 6 | 28-Mar-2000 | Ramsey |
| Montgomery Agnes | 27 | 7 | 9 | 8-Jun-2004 | Ramsey |

| Name | Sec | Lot | Grave | Interment Date | Director |
|---|---|---|---|---|---|
| Montgomery Bobby | 34 | 27 | 6 | 31-Dec-2002 | Ramsey |
| Montgomery Connie | 34 | 42 | 1 | 24-Aug-2009 | Spurlin |
| Montgomery Edd | 27 | 7 | 10 | 27-Feb-2001 | Ramsey |
| Montgomery Flossie | 22 | 11 | 14 | 3-Jan-2000 | Ramsey |
| Montgomery Frances | 27 | 24 | 1 | 28-Mar-1998 | Ramsey |
| Montgomery Harry | 22 | 13 | 15 | 22-Jul-1998 | Ramsey |
| Montgomery Holman | 22 | 11 | 15 | 13-Feb-1996 | Ramsey |
| Montgomery Hubert | 20 | 38 | 16 | 25-Jan-1999 | Ramsey |
| Montgomery Lydia | 29 | 37 | 10 | 2-Jun-1999 | Ramsey |
| Montgomery Thomas | 16 | 56 | 7 | 10-Mar-2010 | Spurlin |
| Montgomery Vernal | 16 | 56 | 6 | 16-Aug-2007 | Spurlin |
| Moody Lorianna | 30 | 77 | 3 | 25-Apr-2003 | Spurlin |
| Moore Anita | 20 | 45 | 13 | 7-Jul-1997 | Ramsey |
| Moore Helen | 23 | 21 | 8 | 22-May-1995 | Ramsey |
| Moore Raymon | 23 | 21 | 4 | 16-Sep-1999 | Ramsey |
| Moore Sadie | 26 | 7 | 13 | 31-Oct-1997 | Ramsey |
| Morford Paul | 30 | 141 | 1 | 21-Aug-2004 | Spurlin |
| Morford Raymond | 30 | 48 | 2 | 14-Feb-2004 | Spurlin |
| Morford Sadie | 30 | 48 | 1 | 14-Jul-1999 | Ramsey |
| Morgan Marie | 30 | 64 | 5 | 4-Nov-1997 | Ramsey |
| Morgan Michael | 36 | 23 | 4 | 21-Jun-2010 | Spurlin |
| Morgan Pauline | 30 | 65 | 7 | 29-May-1998 | Ramsey |
| Morris Billie | 30 | 110 | 6 | 25-Jul-2008 | Spurlin |
| Morris C. William | 16 | 34 | 6 | 30-Dec-2002 | Ramsey |
| Morris Harold | 7 | 41 | 14 | 29-Oct-1997 | Fox |
| Morris Mary | 16 | 34 | 12 | 22-Dec-2005 | Ramsey |
| Morris Stella | 23 | 36 | 16 | 29-Dec-2001 | Ramsey |
| Moser R. Elizabeth | 29A | 103 | 1 | 2-Dec-2009 | Spurlin |

| Name | Sec | Lot | Grave | Interment Date | Director |
|---|---|---|---|---|---|
| Moser William | 29A | 103 | 2 | 20-Sep-2003 | Kerr Bros |
| Moss Berdeaux | 29 | 2 | 1 | 11-Dec-2006 | Ramsey |
| Moss Julian (Jr.) | 32 | 22 | 4 | 4-Feb-2010 | Ramsey |
| Moss Julian (Sr) | 32 | 22 | 8 | 15-Nov-2003 | Spurlin |
| Moss Patrick | 32 | 23 | 1 | 16-Apr-2010 | Ramsey |
| Mucci Ruby | 32 | 12 | 5 | 19-Nov-2009 | Rogers |
| Mulcahy Maymie | 17 | 13 | 14 | 19-Apr-2001 | Prewitt |
| Murphy Alexis | 28 | 10 | 2 | 15-Oct-2001 | Spurlin |
| Murphy Bailey | 29A | 100 | 4 | 19-Sep-2005 | Ramsey |
| Murphy Bessie | 30 | 133 | 7 | 10-Feb-2004 | Spurlin |
| Murphy Buford | 29A | 46 | 2 | 26-Jan-1998 | Spurlin |
| Murphy Canaan | 33 | 19 | 7 | 9-Dec-2004 | Ramsey |
| Murphy Charlie | 12 | 16 | 10 | 18-Jul-1995 | Stith |
| Murphy Frances | 29A | 46 | 1 | 21-Jun-2008 | Spurlin |
| Murphy Joe | 33 | 45 | 8 | 25-Jan-1996 | Ramsey |
| Murphy Kara | 28 | 10 | 1 | 17-Oct-2007 | Spurlin |
| Murphy Lonard | 30 | 113 | 8 | 18-Jun-2002 | Ramsey |
| Murphy Loyd | 33 | 19 | 8 | 14-Oct-1995 | Ramsey |
| Murphy Lucian | 30 | 99 | 6 | 15-Aug-1995 | Ramsey |
| Murphy Mae Jesse | 30 | 113 | 7 | 21-Feb-2002 | Ramsey |
| Murphy Martha | 29A | 105 | 5 | 18-Dec-2007 | Spurlin |
| Murphy Mildred | 30 | 147 | 3 | 21-Apr-2006 | Ramsey |
| Murphy Pauline | 12 | 16 | 9 | 3-Jan-2007 | Stith |
| Murray Robert | 10 | 20 | 15 | 29-Sep-2007 | Alexander |
| Nammack Dorothy | 11 | 25 | 3 | 17-Oct-2003 | |
| Naylor Barbara | 29A | 83 | 3 | 27-May-2009 | Ramsey |
| Naylor Bell Nora | 29 | 113 | 7 | 5-Dec-1995 | Ramsey |
| Naylor Ben | 12 | 2 | 2 | 29-May-2007 | Ramsey |

| Name | Sec | Lot | Grave | Interment Date | Director |
|------|-----|-----|-------|----------------|----------|
| Naylor C. John | 29A | 82 | 1 | 6-Oct-2006 | Ramsey |
| Naylor Della | 22 | 9 | 13 | 13-Jan-2010 | Ramsey |
| Naylor Della Maggie | 28 | 18 | 10 | 20-Oct-1999 | Ramsey |
| Naylor Dorothy | 21 | 24 | 10 | 28-May-2003 | Ramsey |
| Naylor Dow Wolford | 29A | 86 | 5 | 28-Oct-1995 | Ramsey |
| Naylor George (Jr) | 30 | 78 | 4 | 5-Aug-2003 | Spurlin |
| Naylor Gertrude | 12 | 2 | 1 | 14-Jun-2000 | Ramsey |
| Naylor H. Virginia | 30 | 174 | 7 | 3-Dec-2005 | Ramsey |
| Naylor Hazel | 29A | 41 | 7 | 8-Sep-1995 | Milward |
| Naylor Minnie | 29A | 85 | 5 | 23-Jan-2006 | Ramsey |
| Naylor Olivia | 30 | 36 | 3 | 10-Sep-2008 | Ramsey |
| Naylor Orville | 29A | 113 | 2 | 9-Jul-1997 | Ramsey |
| Naylor P. O. | 21 | 6 | 15 | 18-May-1995 | Ramsey |
| Naylor William | 29A | 85 | 6 | 4-Nov-1996 | Ramsey |
| Neely Edna | 30 | 108 | 3 | 11-Aug-2010 | Spurlin |
| Nelson Anthony | 33 | 48 | 6 | 9-Aug-1999 | Spurlin |
| Nevius L. Margaret | 23 | 16 | 14 | 12-Apr-2005 | Spurlin |
| Newby Arnold | 30 | 169 | 8 | 21-Sep-2010 | Ramsey |
| Newby Evelyn | 30 | 73 | 5 | 28-Aug-2007 | Ramsey |
| Newby Jean Norma | 30 | 169 | 7 | 14-May-1997 | Ramsey |
| Newby Landrum | 30 | 73 | 6 | 17-Mar-2001 | Ramsey |
| Newton M. Vergie | 18 | 38 | 6 | 29-May-2010 | Spurlin |
| Nicholas Theodore | 29A | 136 | 6 | 22-Apr-2009 | Ramsey |
| Nieblas F. Mae Edna | 7 | 30 | 1 | 23-Jan-2006 | Spurlin |
| Noe Mike (Jr.) | 29A | 130 | 1 | 10-Feb-2003 | Ramsey |
| Noel Doris | 29A | 112 | 1 | 22-Sep-2000 | Ramsey |
| Noel Mary | 14 | 25 | 10 | 8-Jan-2003 | Spurlin |
| Noel Raymond | 12 | 13 | 8 | 10-Sep-1997 | Ramsey |

| Name | Sec | Lot | Grave | Interment Date | Director |
|------|-----|-----|-------|----------------|----------|
| Oakes Edna | 12 | 30 | 9 | 2-Nov-1995 | Ramsey |
| Oakes Grace | 19 | 23 | 10 | 10-Aug-1996 | Fox |
| Oakes M. Helen | 34 | 5 | 1 | 20-Sep-2003 | |
| Oliver Ann Edith | 30 | 159 | 1 | 16-May-1997 | Ramsey |
| Oliver Della | 33 | 38 | 3 | 23-Jan-1998 | Ramsey |
| Oliver Doris | 30 | 127 | 3 | 18-Jul-1997 | Ramsey |
| Oliver Geneva | 30 | 128 | 5 | 13-Oct-2008 | Ramsey |
| Oliver Jewell | 30 | 128 | 1 | 18-Jan-2000 | Ramsey |
| Oliver Laverana | 30 | 128 | 6 | 10-May-2001 | Ramsey |
| Oliver Zora | 33 | 38 | 4 | 24-Jun-2010 | Ramsey |
| Osmanski John | 1 | 19 | 1 | 28-Oct-1999 | |
| Osmanski Margaret | 1 | 19 | 1 | 3-Mar-1999 | |
| Owen C. Madge | 9 | 6 | 15 | 21-Sep-2006 | Ramsey |
| Owsley E. Mary | 1 | 1 | 16 | 10-Sep-1997 | Ramsey |
| Padgett Jackie | 30 | 134 | 4 | 8-Feb-1997 | Spurlin |
| Palmer Alice | 25 | 23 | 7 | 14-Apr-1997 | Jones |
| Palmer William | 25 | 23 | 11 | 22-Mar-1999 | Lakes |
| Parson Franklin | 1 | 17 | 11 | 19-Feb-1999 | Ramsey |
| Parson Geraldine | 29A | 114 | 7 | 3-Feb-2007 | Spurlin |
| Parson Gilbert | 29A | 120 | 6 | 26-Jul-1995 | Ramsey |
| Parson Lemorris | 29A | 114 | 8 | 19-Dec-2001 | Spurlin |
| Parson Matilda | 29A | 120 | 5 | 9-Nov-2002 | Ramsey |
| Paterson Roy (Jr.) | 28 | 10 | 12 | 4-Oct-2006 | Spurlin |
| Peed C. Beulah | 18 | 19 | 1 | 28-Jan-2006 | Crown Hill |
| Peed Russell | 18 | 19 | 2 | 8-Dec-2007 | Family Funeral Care |
| Peel Dallas | 32 | 5 | 4 | 8-Dec-2003 | McNight |

| Name | Sec | Lot | Grave | Interment Date | Director |
|---|---|---|---|---|---|
| Peel Florence | 30 | 83 | 5 | 20-Apr-2005 | Ramsey |
| Peel Grace | 18 | 39 | 5 | 23-Nov-2002 | Ramsey |
| Peel R. Doris | 23 | 31 | 3 | 29-Dec-2009 | Best & West |
| Peel Thomas | 23 | 31 | 4 | 9-Aug-1995 | Best & West |
| Pence Adam (Jr.) | 27 | 13 | 14 | 14-Jan-2004 | Spurlin |
| Penchoff John | 33 | 47 | 6 | 24-Aug-2006 | Spurlin |
| Pendelton Jesse | 21 | 8 | 7 | 11-Feb-1997 | Ramsey |
| Pendelton Roy | 23 | 116 | 7 | 7-May-1997 | Ramsey |
| Perkins Mayme | 1 | 7 | 16 | 13-Apr-1996 | |
| Peters Pamela | 34 | 26 | 5 | 18-Jun-2009 | Ramsey |
| Petters Elizabeth | 2 | 27 | 9 | 20-Apr-2002 | |
| Petters Nadine | 17 | 5 | 13 | 16-Apr-2003 | Milward |
| Pettus William | 17 | 5 | 12 | 2-Jan-1997 | Milward |
| Pflum Ruth | 33 | 19 | 3 | 24-Feb-2004 | Spurlin |
| Phillips Elizabeth | 25 | 34 | 10 | 10-May-1997 | Ramsey |
| Phillips Maybelle | 22 | 6 | 3 | 31-Mar-2003 | Ramsey |
| Pilcher Ernest | 30 | 114 | 6 | 17-May-2001 | Barnett |
| Pinchoff Mary | 33 | 47 | 5 | 9-Jan-1997 | Ramsey |
| Pinson Dorothy | 14 | 9 | 7 | 17-Sep-2004 | Ramsey |
| Pinson Paul | 14 | 9 | 16 | 31-May-2002 | Ramsey |
| Pixley Jane | 29A | 63 | 5 | 14-Jul-2009 | Spurlin |
| Pixley Keith | 29A | 63 | 6 | 23-Aug-2004 | Stith |
| Playforth Charlotte | 33 | 2 | 7 | 28-Dec-2009 | Ramsey |
| Playforth Mitchell | 34 | 369 | 6 | 8-Feb-2006 | Spurlin |
| Plummer Brandon | 34 | 31 | 2 | 22-Jan-2009 | McNight |
| Plummer Carlton | 30 | 77 | 1 | 3-Jun-1995 | Ramsey |
| Plummer Louise | 30 | 76 | 4 | 17-Feb-2010 | Ramsey |
| Pollard Bulah | 20 | 46 | 3 | 22-Sep-2000 | Ramsey |

| Name | Sec | Lot | Grave | Interment Date | Director |
|---|---|---|---|---|---|
| Pollard Denny Robert | 30 | 105 | 4 | 4-May-1995 | Ramsey |
| Pollard Eugene | 11 | 5 | 13 | 9-Aug-2008 | Spurlin |
| Pollard Geneva | 30 | 105 | 3 | 7-Jan-2003 | Spurlin |
| Pollard Lucy | 27 | 25 | 2 | 7-Feb-2002 | Ramsey |
| Pollard Mabel | 30 | 50 | 5 | 8-Oct-2003 | Ramsey |
| Pollard Margaret | 23 | 38 | 3 | 28-Sep-1996 | Ramsey |
| Pollard Virgil | 30 | 105 | 8 | 6-Oct-1995 | Ramsey |
| Porter Janet | 30 | 184 | 3 | 31-Mar-1999 | Ramsey |
| Porter John | 30 | 184 | 2 | 7-Jan-2000 | Alexander |
| Potts F. Anna | 29 | 11 | 5 | 30-Nov-2005 | Spurlin |
| Powell Claude | 21 | 4 | 13 | 14-Jan-1998 | Ramsey |
| Powell Minnie | 21 | 4 | 7 | 7-Feb-2009 | Spurlin |
| Powell Morgan | 33 | 35 | 4 | 18-Apr-1998 | Spurlin |
| Powell Sada | 33 | 35 | 3 | 22-Oct-2010 | Spurlin |
| Powers Cecil | 20 | 34 | 10 | 13-Sep-2005 | Spurlin |
| Powers N. Henrietta | 33 | 7 | 1 | 15-Mar-2010 | Ramsey |
| Poynter B. Dana | 24 | 11 | 4 | 2-Oct-2010 | Spurlin |
| Poynter D. S. | 24 | 11 | 2 | 14-Feb-2000 | Spurlin |
| Poynter John | 30 | 62 | 2 | 29-Jun-2004 | Spurlin |
| Poynter Leslie | 33 | 31 | 4 | 17-May-1999 | Ramsey |
| Poynter Marie | 33 | 31 | 3 | 23-Jan-1999 | Ramsey |
| Prather Collis | 11 | 21 | 3 | 10-Jan-2002 | Ramsey |
| Prather Gary | 29 | 27 | 11 | 27-Dec-1997 | |
| Prather Mabel | 20 | 12 | 6 | 5-May-2000 | Johnson |
| Preston Annie | 27 | 31 | 14 | 27-Mar-1995 | Ramsey |
| Preston B. Willie | 24 | 19 | 3 | 18-Feb-1997 | Ramsey |
| Preston Eloise | 30 | 129 | 3 | 25-Nov-2009 | Spurlin |
| Preston Emily | 31 | 6 | 6 | 19-Feb-2003 | Ramsey |

| Name | Sec | Lot | Grave | Interment Date | Director |
|---|---|---|---|---|---|
| Preston Eugene | 29 | 12 | 3 | 16-Jan-2006 | Ramsey |
| Preston George | 24 | 19 | 6 | 8-Jul-2004 | Ramsey |
| Preston Harry | 24 | 19 | 14 | 7-Jan-2009 | Ramsey |
| Preston Hubert | 27 | 31 | 15 | 13-Jul-1998 | Ramsey |
| Preston Joe | 31 | 6 | 8 | 5-Dec-2005 | Ramsey |
| Preston Lee Eva | 27 | 16 | 11 | 10-May-1995 | Ramsey |
| Preston Marjorie | 29 | 12 | 2 | 28-Dec-2005 | Ramsey |
| Preston Mary | 30 | 28 | 3 | 22-Aug-1995 | Ramsey |
| Preston Nellie | 30 | 149 | 1 | 7-Jun-2010 | Best & West |
| Preston Sylvia | 24 | 2 | 15 | 7-Feb-1997 | Ramsey |
| Prewitt Alene | 29A | 133 | 5 | 4-Aug-2008 | Spurlin |
| Prewitt Allan | 29A | 122 | 2 | 8-Nov-2006 | Spurlin |
| Prewitt Allene | 27 | 28 | 6 | 24-Dec-1999 | Ramsey |
| Prewitt Amanda | 30 | 167 | 7 | 22-Aug-2001 | Spurlin |
| Prewitt Arthur | 30 | 167 | 8 | 14-Dec-2004 | Spurlin |
| Prewitt Berl Wilford | 21 | 16 | 8 | 17-Apr-2001 | Johnson |
| Prewitt Betty | 26 | 3 | 14 | 30-Oct-2003 | Combs |
| Prewitt Callie | 33 | 39 | 4 | 18-Jul-1998 | Ramsey |
| Prewitt Clellan | 21 | 12 | 12 | 10-Sep-2001 | Pulaski |
| Prewitt Delbert | 26 | 7 | 6 | 25-Nov-1995 | Ramsey |
| Prewitt Elmer | 21 | 31 | 2 | 18-Jul-1996 | Ramsey |
| Prewitt Emma | 21 | 31 | 1 | 20-Dec-2010 | Spurlin |
| Prewitt Forest | 30 | 4 | 6 | 23-Apr-1996 | Ramsey |
| Prewitt H. J. | 23 | 25 | 4 | 31-Aug-2000 | Ramsey |
| Prewitt James | 33 | 41 | 8 | 11-May-1996 | Ramsey |
| Prewitt Leora | 21 | 12 | 11 | 7-Mar-2007 | Pulaski |
| Prewitt Lola | 29A | 131 | 1 | 16-Apr-2001 | Ramsey |
| Prewitt Lucy | 23 | 25 | 3 | 17-Jun-2004 | Ramsey |

| Name | Sec | Lot | Grave | Interment Date | Director |
|---|---|---|---|---|---|
| Prewitt Nathan | 27 | 28 | 7 | 1-Oct-2001 | Ramsey |
| Prewitt Oda | 21 | 16 | 13 | 23-May-1997 | Oldman |
| Prewitt Sharon | 30 | 175 | 3 | 26-Jun-1998 | Ramsey |
| Prewitt Turner Annie | 5 | 6 | 11 | 13-Aug-1997 | Duell Clark |
| Price Carl | 33 | 15 | 4 | 6-Oct-1998 | Ramsey |
| Price Dora | 30 | 91 | 7 | 17-Sep-2007 | Oldham |
| Price Jalie | 33 | 15 | 3 | 23-Oct-2000 | Ramsey |
| Proffett Cobb Lida | 27 | 3 | 15 | 27-Dec-1999 | Ramsey |
| Puckett Lyda | 30 | 137 | 1 | 26-Jan-2006 | Ramsey |
| Purcell Agnes | 34 | 48 | 7 | 17-Sep-2008 | Spurlin |
| Ragan Doug | 28 | 22 | 23 | 3-May-2008 | Spurlin |
| Ragan George | 7 | 26 | 16 | 21-Jan-2006 | Spurlin |
| Ragan Nancy | 18 | 36 | 15 | 5-Nov-2004 | Hodapp |
| Raines Katie | 23 | 40 | 77 | 2-Apr-1999 | Ramsey |
| Raines Mae Della | 23 | 40 | 15 | 4-Dec-2007 | Ramsey |
| Ramsey Hazel | 33 | 28 | 7 | 31-Mar-1997 | Ramsey |
| Ramsey Jim | 29A | 118 | 4 | 29-Nov-2000 | Ramsey |
| Rankin Allen | 18 | 16 | 15 | 6-Jun-2002 | |
| Rankin Bessie | 32 | 44 | 1 | 28-Dec-2010 | Spurlin |
| Rankin Betty | 32 | 44 | 5 | 31-Jan-2000 | Ramsey |
| Rankin Farris James | 32 | 27 | 6 | 23-Jun-2000 | Spurlin |
| Rankin Lee James | 30 | 52 | 2 | 12-Dec-1997 | Ramsey |
| Rankin Lee John | 32 | 44 | 2 | 26-Jan-2008 | Spurlin |
| Rankin Lee Robert | 30 | 52 | 6 | 13-Jun-1997 | Ramsey |
| Rankin Lou Mary | 29A | 55 | 7 | 12-Jan-2000 | Spurlin |
| Rankin Nannie | 32 | 27 | 5 | 2-Jun-2000 | Spurlin |
| Ratcliffe James | 24 | 28 | 1 | 2-Apr-2003 | Ramsey |
| Ratcliffe Martha | 24 | 28 | 2 | 11-Oct-2010 | Ramsey |

| Name | Sec | Lot | Grave | Interment Date | Director |
|------|-----|-----|-------|----------------|----------|
| Ray Billy | 18 | 7 | 12 | 24-Mar-2007 | Ramsey |
| Ray C. Jean | 30 | 63 | 8 | 11-Apr-2007 | Spurlin |
| Ray Charles | 9 | 27 | 10 | 15-Apr-1996 | Ramsey |
| Ray Charles | 29A | 96 | 6 | 29-Jan-2007 | Spurlin |
| Ray D. J. | 33 | 12 | 3 | 16-Oct-1999 | Spurlin |
| Ray D. William | 25 | 18 | 10 | 26-Mar-2001 | Spurlin |
| Ray Doreen | 18 | 7 | 9 | 24-Jun-1996 | Ramsey |
| Ray Edward | 20 | 18 | 3 | 12-Nov-2003 | Ramsey |
| Ray Elizabeth | 29A | 104 | 7 | 25-Mar-1996 | Ramsey |
| Ray Elsie | 33 | 12 | 7 | 20-Jan-1997 | Ramsey |
| Ray G. Harold | 16 | 12 | 4 | 2-Sep-2009 | Spurlin |
| Ray H. Nora | 30 | 20 | 5 | 2-Nov-2009 | Spurlin |
| Ray Helen | 33 | 12 | 4 | 14-Sep-2004 | Spurlin |
| Ray Homer | 33 | 9 | 1 | 20-Feb-1998 | Spurlin |
| Ray Janie Sara | 27 | 19X | 1 | 5-Apr-1996 | Ramsey |
| Ray Julian | 29 | 2 | 6 | 22-May-1996 | Ramsey |
| Ray L. Helen | 21 | 30 | 6 | 27-May-2008 | Kerr Bros |
| Ray Larry | 25 | 42 | 10 | 11-Mar-2010 | Ramsey |
| Ray Lucille | 25 | 18 | 14 | 26-Jul-2001 | Spurlin |
| Ray Mabel | 30 | 87 | 4 | 25-Jul-2001 | Spurlin |
| Ray Mary | 33 | 30 | 7 | 23-Jul-1997 | Ramsey |
| Ray Michael | 20 | 23 | 15 | 8-May-2002 | Ramsey |
| Ray Nancy | 7 | 5 | 13 | 3-Dec-2004 | Spurlin |
| Ray Nannie | 30 | 148 | 7 | 16-Dec-2003 | Ramsey |
| Ray Nellie | 21 | 18 | 15 | 7-Mar-2002 | Ramsey |
| Ray Patricia | 30 | 167 | 1 | 8-Feb-2010 | Spurlin |
| Ray Royce | 26 | 20 | 8 | 28-May-2001 | Ramsey |
| Ray Stewart | 20 | 18 | 8 | 17-Mar-2006 | Ramsey |

| Name | Sec | Lot | Grave | Interment Date | Director |
|------|-----|-----|-------|----------------|----------|
| Ray T. Elmer (Jr.) | 16 | 53 | 13 | 21-May-2005 | Ramsey |
| Rayburn Frank John | 9 | 3 | 3 | 19-Sep-2000 | Ramsey |
| Reed Bertie | 27 | 20 | 15 | 21-May-1998 | Ramsey |
| Reed Gordon | 12 | 31 | 15 | 29-Mar-2004 | Stith |
| Reed Minnie | 12 | 31 | 14 | 14-Jan-2004 | Stith |
| Reed Oscar | 27 | 20 | 16 | 28-May-2001 | Ramsey |
| Reeves James | 33 | 31 | 7 | 27-Apr-1996 | Ramsey |
| Reynolds Clay | 29A | 137 | 3 | 25-Mar-2000 | Spurlin |
| Reynolds G. Flora | 29A | 50 | 3 | 25-Feb-2005 | Ramsey |
| Reynolds Leroy | 29A | 50 | 4 | 1-May-2002 | Ramsey |
| Reynolds Lucille | 29A | 137 | 4 | 5-Sep-2002 | Spurlin |
| Reynolds Mabel | 16 | 55 | 11 | 18-Jan-2002 | Spurlin |
| Reynolds Ray | 16 | 55 | 12 | 14-Dec-2002 | Ramsey |
| Rhodes Bessie | 18 | 4 | 10 | 15-Apr-2003 | Kerr Bros |
| Rhodes Jessie | 33 | 39 | 1 | 27-Mar-2003 | Ramsey |
| Rhodus Ethel | 16 | 40 | 9 | 12-Feb-2008 | Ramsey |
| Rhodus Woody | 21 | 28 | 16 | 13-Oct-2010 | Spurlin |
| Rice Lee Mary | 25 | 29 | 3 | 28-Mar-1997 | Ramsey |
| Rich Edna | 25 | 41 | 11 | 26-Apr-2003 | Ramsey |
| Rich Helen | 30 | 36 | 5 | 9-Mar-1998 | Ramsey |
| Rich M. Anna | 29A | 67 | 3 | 30-Jan-2006 | Ramsey |
| Richardson Eugene | 11 | 36 | 3 | 17-Jan-2009 | Ramsey |
| Richardson G. Candace | 20 | 32 | 9 | 19-Jul-2010 | Ramsey |
| Richardson James | 34 | 47 | 6 | 3-Jan-2004 | Ramsey |
| Richardson Mary | 34 | 24 | 4 | 24-May-2004 | Ramsey |
| Richardson Millard | 29 | 31 | 9 | 6-Oct-1995 | Ramsey |
| Richardson T. Minnie | 34 | 47 | 5 | 24-Mar-2009 | Spurlin |
| Rigsby Ethel | 30 | 172 | 5 | 22-Feb-1999 | Ramsey |

| Name | Sec | Lot | Grave | Interment Date | Director |
|---|---|---|---|---|---|
| Rigsby Lewis | 30 | 160 | 8 | 20-Jun-2009 | Spurlin |
| Roach Nell | 17 | 31 | 10 | 14-Apr-2005 | Spurlin |
| Roark Edward | 25 | 25 | 10 | 21-Oct-2000 | Ramsey |
| Robbins Burgess | 30 | 78 | 6 | 5-Aug-2005 | Ramsey |
| Robbins Louise | 30 | 78 | 5 | 31-Mar-2006 | Ramsey |
| Robinson Hazel | 33 | 28 | 5 | 18-May-1999 | Ramsey |
| Robinson Johnny | 30 | 155 | 8 | 8-Feb-2003 | Ramsey |
| Robinson Lewis | 23 | 28 | 6 | 24-Sep-1998 | Ramsey |
| Robinson Shirley | 20 | 52 | 4 | 20-Oct-2008 | Ramsey |
| Rodney Cynthia | 34 | 15 | 5 | 10-Apr-2007 | Spurlin |
| Roger C. James | 23 | 15 | 15 | 9-Jul-1997 | Ramsey |
| Rogers Betty | 30 | 112 | 3 | 2-Sep-1995 | Ramsey |
| Rogers Gladys | 18 | 33 | 11 | 20-Mar-2004 | Ramsey |
| Rogers J. Mary | 27 | 13 | 15 | 28-Jan-2004 | Spurlin |
| Rogers J. Nathaniel (Jr.) | 32 | 22 | 6 | 5-Feb-2005 | Spurlin |
| Rogers Lee J. | 16 | 5 | 14 | 26-Sep-2008 | Ramsey |
| Rogers Lucille | 30 | 135 | 3 | 25-Jan-2001 | Ramsey |
| Rogers Morris | 27 | 13 | 16 | 28-Dec-1999 | Spurlin |
| Rose James | 17 | 21 | 8 | 14-Feb-2004 | Milward |
| Ross Bobby | 34 | 6 | 2 | 16-May-2003 | Spurlin |
| Ross Georgia | 28 | 18 | 5 | 11-Nov-1996 | Milward |
| Ross Margaret | 29A | 84 | 7 | 10-Jul-1999 | Ramsey |
| Ross Samuel | 32 | 29 | 3 | 18-May-2009 | Spurlin |
| Ruble Clara | 18 | 40 | 3 | 27-Jan-1999 | Ramsey |
| Ruble Thelma | 17 | 6 | 10 | 25-Nov-1998 | Arch L. Hardy |
| Russel Willard | 30 | 4 | 8 | 28-Sep-1996 | Ramsey |
| Sallee Ralph | 34 | 56 | 6 | 29-Jan-2009 | Ramsey |

| Name | Sec | Lot | Grave | Interment Date | Director |
|---|---|---|---|---|---|
| Sanders Cecil | 32 | 30 | 2 | 16-Jan-2007 | Spurlin |
| Sanders Florence | 26 | 6 | 11 | 2-Nov-2001 | Spurlin |
| Sanders H. Willie | 25 | 26 | 13 | 26-Feb-1997 | Ramsey |
| Sanders Helen | 25 | 26 | 12 | 21-Mar-1996 | Ramsey |
| Sanders Stanley | 25 | 20 | 16 | 30-Nov-1998 | Preston Pruitt |
| Sargent P. Allen | 33 | 3 | 7 | 21-Feb-2006 | Ramsey |
| Satterly Lillie | 33 | 54 | 1 | 27-Jul-2001 | Spurlin |
| Satterly Ralph | 33 | 54 | 2 | 11-Oct-2004 | Spurlin |
| Saylor B. Marjorie | 30 | 88 | 7 | 23-Apr-2007 | Ramsey |
| Saylor Fannie | 33 | 52 | 2 | 6-Jul-2000 | Ramsey |
| Saylor Homer | 27 | 21 | 8 | 4-Feb-1997 | Oldman |
| Schooler Dorothy | 29A | 66 | 2 | 12-Dec-1995 | Ramsey |
| Schooler Grover | 29A | 66 | 3 | 27-Dec-1996 | Ramsey |
| Schooler Jean | 25 | 22 | 10 | 24-Apr-2000 | Cole & Garrett |
| Schooler Paul | 25 | 22 | 10 | 12-Jul-1999 | Spurlin |
| Scott Bernice | 25 | 21 | 4 | 29-Oct-1997 | Ramsey |
| Scott Betty | 16 | 56 | 3 | 6-Jul-2005 | Ramsey |
| Scott David | 11 | 2 | 16 | 17-Apr-2004 | Spurlin |
| Scott Ebbie | 29A | 55 | 4 | 20-Mar-2009 | Ramsey |
| Scott Ethel | 30 | 10 | 4 | 13-Mar-2000 | Ramsey |
| Scott Lettie | 26 | 15 | 11 | 8-Dec-1998 | Ramsey |
| Scott Louella | 29A | 55 | 3 | 22-Dec-2003 | Ramsey |
| Scott M. Lois | 29A | 55 | 8 | 23-Jun-2005 | Spurlin |
| Scott M. Mary | 16 | 56 | 11 | 15-Nov-2002 | Ramsey |
| Scott Mae Stella | 16 | 11 | 10 | 12-Apr-1996 | Ransdell |
| Sebastian Bluford | 24 | 5 | 2 | 13-Mar-2004 | Ramsey |

| Name | Sec | Lot | Grave | Interment Date | Director |
|---|---|---|---|---|---|
| Sebastian Chester | 22 | 17 | 13 | 3-Dec-2002 | Ramsey |
| Sebastian Colman | 20 | 50 | 10 | 31-Oct-1996 | Ramsey |
| Sebastian Emmett | 17 | 11 | 2 | 2-Mar-1999 | Ramsey |
| Sebastian Fannie | 29 | 14 | 6 | 31-Oct-1998 | Ramsey |
| Sebastian Gracie | 22 | 17 | 12 | 15-Nov-2004 | Ramsey |
| Sebastian Helen | 29A | 133 | 7 | 12-Jul-2008 | Ramsey |
| Sebastian Hurte Myrtle | 33 | 14 | 5 | 5-Feb-1999 | Spurlin |
| Sebastian James | 23 | 35 | 3 | 30-Apr-1997 | Ramsey |
| Sebastian James | 30 | 37 | 2 | 28-Apr-2006 | Ramsey |
| Sebastian Loyd | 29A | 62 | 2 | 25-Oct-2004 | Ramsey |
| Sebastian Mable | 20 | 53 | 1 | 3-Jan-1995 | Ramsey |
| Sebastian Marie | 29 | 9 | 2 | 23-Jun-1995 | Ramsey |
| Sebastian Mary | 32 | 29 | 1 | 9-Jul-1999 | Ramsey |
| Sebastian McClellan | 16 | 19 | 6 | 1-Oct-2007 | Spurlin |
| Sebastian Nathan | 32 | 29 | 2 | 27-Mar-2000 | Ramsey |
| Sebastian Ova | 29A | 87 | 5 | 26-Oct-2000 | Ramsey |
| Sebastian Pam | 24 | 5 | 3 | 30-Nov-2002 | Ramsey |
| Sebastian Ruth | 30 | 144 | 1 | 28-Dec-1999 | Ramsey |
| Sebastian Ruth | 29A | 62 | 1 | 10-Apr-2004 | Ramsey |
| Sebastian Tolbert | 26 | 30 | 16 | 8-Sep-1995 | Ramsey |
| Sebastian W. Henry | 29 | 9 | 10 | 1-Mar-2007 | Ramsey |
| Sebastian William | 30 | 144 | 6 | 19-Jan-2010 | Ramsey |
| Sebastian Willie | 24 | 5 | 9 | 20-Dec-2005 | Ramsey |
| Sharp C. Sarah | 25 | 30 | 3 | 14-Jan-2003 | Stith |
| Shearer (Pete) Homer | 33 | 26 | 2 | 28-Jul-1997 | Ramsey |
| Shearer Cecil | 30 | 161 | 6 | 20-Aug-1996 | Ramsey |
| Shearer Donald | 33 | 43 | 5 | 28-Mar-1998 | Ramsey |

| Name | Sec | Lot | Grave | Interment Date | Director |
|---|---|---|---|---|---|
| Shearer Mae | 33 | 26 | 1 | 11-Nov-1996 | Ramsey |
| Shearer Michael | 34 | 56 | 2 | 12-May-2010 | Ramsey |
| Shearer Oscar | 19 | 19 | 2 | 14-Aug-2003 | Ramsey |
| Shearer Pauline | 30 | 167 | 5 | 30-Nov-2010 | Ramsey |
| Shearer Robert | 19 | 22 | 2 | 11-Apr-2009 | Ramsey |
| Shearer William | 7 | 27 | 14 | 18-Apr-2003 | Ramsey |
| Shell Bruce | 18 | 44 | 7 | 26-Dec-1998 | Ramsey |
| Shell Georgia | 18 | 44 | 13 | 7-Aug-2008 | Spurlin |
| Shelly Burnam | 16 | 27 | 7 | 3-Jan-1997 | Ramsey |
| Shelton Harmon | 33 | 17 | 3 | 11-Feb-2004 | McNight |
| Sheperson Mildred | 12 | 5 | 3 | 3-Feb-2003 | Alexander |
| Sherman Edward | 32 | 2 | 5&6 | 24-Dec-2004 | Ramsey |
| Sherrow Coleman (Jr.) | 30 | 154 | 2 | 15-Jun-2006 | Spurlin |
| Sherrow Colman | 30 | 154 | 6 | 13-Nov-1999 | Ramsey |
| Sherrow Helen | 30 | 154 | 5 | 31-Mar-1995 | Fox |
| Sherrow Lorraine | 18 | 28 | 6 | 4-Jan-2008 | Ramsey |
| Sherrow Peachie | 12 | 44 | 4 | 17-Apr-1999 | Preston Pruitt |
| Shockley Bertus | 29 | 13 | 12 | 14-May-1999 | Spurlin |
| Shopman Jean Wilma | 34 | 45 | 3 | 5-May-2010 | Spurlin |
| Shopman Walter | 34 | 45 | 4 | 12-Jul-2010 | Spurlin |
| Short Mae Lillie | 30 | 137 | 3 | 4-Aug-2005 | Ramsey |
| Short Virgina | 32 | 42 | 5 | 26-Jul-2006 | Arnett |
| Sides Paul | 32 | 14 | 2 | 11-Apr-2003 | Ramsey |
| Sigala Paula | 25 | 33 | 15 | 30-Mar-2004 | Ramsey |
| Simpson Bert | 23 | 12 | 12 | 20-Apr-1998 | Spurlin |
| Simpson Cora | 23 | 12 | 15 | 13-Dec-2005 | Spurlin |
| Simpson Elizabeth | 23 | 22 | 15 | 9-Oct-2003 | Ramsey |

| Name | Sec | Lot | Grave | Interment Date | Director |
|---|---|---|---|---|---|
| Simpson H. Harriet | 23 | 22 | 11&12 | 10-May-2002 | |
| Simpson H. Marguerite | 29 | 32 | 10 | 5-Jun-2008 | Kerr Bros |
| Simpson Jane | 29 | 29 | 10 | 12-Oct-2000 | Spurlin |
| Simpson Jewell | 23 | 22 | 1 | 13-Feb-2001 | Ramsey |
| Simpson Lloyd | 23 | 12 | 11 | 14-May-2009 | Spurlin |
| Simpson Lula | 20 | 47 | 8 | 26-Apr-2000 | Ramsey |
| Simpson Velma | 23 | 22 | 11 | 23-Feb-1995 | Ramsey |
| Singleton Kristopher | 31 | 14 | 1 | 2-Dec-2009 | Spurlin |
| Sleake William | 33 | 50 | 2 | 26-Jan-1998 | Ramsey |
| Sloan Mae | 30 | 25 | 5 | 7-Aug-2007 | Kerr Bros |
| Smith B. Matt | 22 | 3 | 8 | 13-Aug-2002 | Spurlin |
| Smith Earl | 33 | 8 | 6 | 12-Nov-2008 | McNight |
| Smith Elwood | 2 | 2 | 13 | 14-Jan-1900 | |
| Smith H. J. | 33 | 23 | 2 | 14-Feb-1996 | Fox |
| Smith Harmon | 30 | 138 | 2 | 20-Jan-2009 | McNight |
| Smith Hazel | 33 | 58 | 6 | 26-Oct-2001 | Ramsey |
| Smith Jesse | 30 | 8 | 6 | 12-Jan-2002 | Spurlin |
| Smith K. Laura | 20 | 28 | 14 | 13-Jul-2009 | Spurlin |
| Smith R. John | 3 | 15 | 13 | 9-Sep-2009 | Spurlin |
| Smith Ruth | 33 | 8 | 5 | 2-Jul-1997 | Ramsey |
| Smith S. Betty | 34 | 57 | 1 | 19-Nov-2005 | Spurlin |
| Smith Waters Nora | 33 | 38 | 16 | 25-Jan-1999 | Spurlin |
| Snyder Effie | 21 | 29 | 3 | 6-Mar-2003 | Ramsey |
| Snyder Patsey | 34 | 61 | 7 | 30-Dec-2008 | Ramsey |
| Souder Herbert | 12 | 30 | 15 | 29-Nov-2001 | Spurlin |
| Sowder A. Shirley | 30 | 124 | 7 | 23-Nov-2005 | B.J. Meyer |
| Sowder Bill | 23 | 15 | 11 | 17-Jan-1996 | Ramsey |
| Sowder Frana | 33 | 30 | 7 | 13-Apr-2010 | Owens |

| Name | Sec | Lot | Grave | Interment Date | Director |
|---|---|---|---|---|---|
| Sowder George | 34 | 18 | 4 | 3-Feb-2003 | Ramsey |
| Sowder Lester | 34 | 19 | 3 | 19-Apr-2010 | Ramsey |
| Sowder Loraine | 29 | 23 | 7 | 24-Mar-2000 | Ramsey |
| Sowder Pearl | 34 | 19 | 2 | 3-Nov-2008 | Ramsey |
| Sparks Beatrice | 18 | 5 | 14 | 15-Oct-2008 | Ramsey |
| Sparks Carl | 18 | 5 | 15 | 6-Jun-2007 | Ramsey |
| Sparks Elisha | 33 | 19 | 2 | 3-Feb-1995 | Ramsey |
| Sparks Hattie | 27 | 9 | 2 | 20-Jan-1996 | Ramsey |
| Sparks Thelma | 29A | 112 | 5 | 27-Oct-1999 | Spurlin |
| Spaulding Hunter | 20 | 60 | 6 | 2-Dec-2003 | Ramsey |
| Speake Lillie | 23 | 18 | 2 | 14-Jun-1996 | Ramsey |
| Speake Lois | 33 | 50 | 1 | 10-May-2004 | Ramsey |
| Speake Margaret | 12 | 9 | 9 | 16-Jan-1996 | Ramsey |
| Speakes Ralph | 23 | 18 | 11 | 24-Oct-2004 | Ramsey |
| Speaks Carl | 21 | 19 | 2 | 24-Jun-1997 | Ramsey |
| Spears Jerry | 33 | 49 | 6 | 5-Mar-2002 | Ramsey |
| Spicer Dorothy | 16 | 27 | 7 | 3-Jan-1997 | Smith |
| Spoonamore Eunice | 30 | 37 | 7 | 27-Feb-2002 | Owens |
| Spurlin A. James | 30 | 94 | 8 | 1-Dec-2007 | Spurlin |
| Stanfield Patty | 33 | 57 | 1 | 26-Jun-2009 | Ramsey |
| Starnes Printus | 34 | 14 | 6 | 23-Jul-2003 | Ramsey |
| Statem Jo Betty | 22 | 24 | 14 | 2-Apr-1996 | |
| Statom May Mary | 16 | 22 | 15 | 8-Feb-1995 | Ramsey |
| Steel Ola | 20 | 35 | 10 | 11-Jun-2001 | |
| Steele G. Mary | 22 | 14 | 16 | 1-Jul-2008 | Spurlin |
| Steffen Jackqueline | 30 | 133 | 5 | 15-May-2001 | Ramsey |
| Stempfly Sherman | 34 | 49 | 6 | 15-Aug-2006 | Ramsey |
| Steven Adam | 33 | 64 | 1 | 14-Aug-2006 | Spurlin |

| Name | Sec | Lot | Grave | Interment Date | Director |
|---|---|---|---|---|---|
| Steven Mae Vera | 30 | 118 | 7 | 25-Mar-2009 | Spurlin |
| Stevens M. Senia | 30 | 64 | 7 | 17-Mar-2001 | Spurlin |
| Stewart Catherine | 9 | 11 | 2 | 7-Aug-1998 | |
| Stewart Thomas | 9 | 11 | 2 | 7-Aug-1998 | |
| Stinetorf LaVerne | 18 | 3 | 12 | 29-Mar-2005 | Ramsey |
| Stinnet Henry | 27 | 15 | 8 | 8-Mar-1999 | Ramsey |
| Stinnett Henry (Jr.) | 30 | 112 | 7 | 6-Jul-2000 | Ramsey |
| Stinnett P. Hattie | 30 | 110 | 7 | 3-Dec-2010 | Ramsey |
| Stipes Evelyn | 30 | 114 | 6 | 17-May-2001 | Ramsey |
| Stipes Holman | 22 | 3 | 16 | 21-Oct-1997 | Spurlin |
| Stocker Linden | 34 | 40 | 8 | 16-Oct-2007 | Spurlin |
| Stone Evelyn | 30 | 111 | 6 | 27-Jul-2009 | Ramsey |
| Stone Gladys | 1 | 35 | 1 | 7-Apr-2005 | Ramsey |
| Stone Homer | 1 | 35 | 2 | 22-Mar-1997 | Ramsey |
| Stone Nan | 30 | 77 | 5 | 5-Dec-1998 | Ramsey |
| Stopp Irvine (Jr.) | 21 | 32 | 4 | 20-Sep-2004 | |
| Stratton Isaac (Jr.) | 30 | 143 | 7 | 12-Jul-2008 | Ramsey |
| Stratton Sadie | 30 | 143 | 5 | 19-Aug-2010 | Ramsey |
| Stump Link | 30 | 145 | 6 | 17-Oct-1995 | Ramsey |
| Sturgill Ann | 34 | 38 | 2 | 30-Nov-2002 | Spurlin |
| Surber Cora | 27 | 20 | 3 | 1-Nov-2001 | Young |
| Surber Parker | 21 | 31 | 14 | 24-Apr-1997 | Ramsey |
| Sutton C. Odus | 18 | 34 | 12 | 29-Jan-1997 | Ramsey |
| Sutton Eddie (Jr.) | 23 | 38 | 2 | 20-Oct-2009 | Ramsey |
| Sutton Edna | 22 | 19 | 14 | 28-Mar-2008 | Ramsey |
| Sutton Elizabeth | 18 | 34 | 11 | 18-Dec-2001 | Ramsey |
| Sutton Ernest | 22 | 16 | 11 | 16-Nov-2005 | Ramsey |
| Sutton Ethel | 22 | 16 | 10 | 6-Mar-2001 | Ramsey |

| Name | Sec | Lot | Grave | Interment Date | Director |
|---|---|---|---|---|---|
| Sutton Evelyn | 23 | 38 | 9 | 11-Nov-2002 | Ramsey |
| Sutton Helen | 29A | 99 | 3 | 23-May-1995 | Ramsey |
| Sutton Jeremy | 23 | 23 | 33 | 16-Oct-2000 | Spurlin |
| Sutton Kathleen | 22 | 16 | 1 | 2-Jan-1997 | Ramsey |
| Sutton Louis | 16 | 17 | 6 | 21-Apr-1997 | Ramsey |
| Sutton Sallie | 29A | 114 | 3 | 8-Jun-2001 | Spurlin |
| Sutton William | 23 | 38 | 16 | 10-Oct-2003 | Ramsey |
| Sutton William | 32 | 9 | 3 | 7-Mar-2005 | Spurlin |
| Swope Edna | 23 | 23 | 8 | 25-Mar-2003 | Ramsey |
| Swope Robert | 16 | 7 | 2 | 23-Feb-1998 | Ramsey |
| Tankersley Andrew | 30 | 92 | 1 | 28-Jan-1998 | Ramsey |
| Tankersley Loyd | 24 | 14 | 16 | 20-Mar-1995 | Ramsey |
| Tapp George | 15 | 6 | 7 | 28-Oct-2004 | Stith |
| Tapp Lillian | 30 | 21 | 5 | 19-Apr-2010 | Spurlin |
| Tatem V. William | 22 | 24 | 14 | 12-Mar-2007 | Williams |
| Taylor H. Mattie | 27 | 3 | 13 | 5-May-2007 | Ramsey |
| Teater Bernard | 30 | 113 | 6 | 2-May-1997 | Spurlin |
| Teater Betty | 34 | 18 | 1 | 24-Aug-2005 | Ramsey |
| Teater Ernest | 28 | 4 | 12 | 1-Apr-2001 | |
| Teater Geneva | 20 | 51 | 2 | 22-Dec-1997 | Spurlin |
| Teater Janice | 29 | 18 | 9 | 3-Nov-2010 | Spurlin |
| Teater Juanita | 29 | 18 | 8 | 19-Jul-2000 | Spurlin |
| Teater Margaret | 28 | 4 | 10 | 21-Dec-2007 | Spurlin |
| Teater Margaret Anna | 11 | 10 | 12 | 6-Aug-1997 | Spurlin |
| Teater Myra | 29 | 5 | 15 | 15-Feb-2003 | Ramsey |
| Teater Ruby | 30 | 113 | 5 | 23-Oct-2007 | Spurlin |
| Teater Stella | 29 | 18 | 2 | 15-Nov-2006 | Ramsey |
| Teater Susan | 34 | 16 | 5 | 28-Jan-2010 | Ramsey |

| Name | Sec | Lot | Grave | Interment Date | Director |
|---|---|---|---|---|---|
| Teater William | 28 | 4 | 1 | 15-May-2006 | Spurlin |
| Thomas Beulah | 9 | 13 | 9 | 16-May-2005 | Spurlin |
| Thomas Vivian | 9 | 13 | 10 | 9-Feb-2002 | Spurlin |
| Thompson Carl | 30 | 26 | 8 | 24-Nov-2008 | Spurlin |
| Thompson G. Nora | 23 | 19 | * | 14-Apr-2010 | |
| Thompson K. Maurice | 20 | 14 | 7 | 21-Jan-1995 | Ramsey |
| Thompson Raymond (Jr.) | 30 | 49 | 5 | 14-May-2007 | Spurlin |
| Thompson Ruby | 20 | 14 | 6 | 19-Mar-1999 | Spurlin |
| Traver Margaret | 33 | 55 | 8 | 26-May-1998 | Ramsey |
| Tribble Roberta | 16 | 37 | 1 | 26-Nov-2002 | Spurlin |
| Tucker Jonathon | 33 | 42 | 1 | 25-Jul-1995 | Ramsey |
| Tudor Buford | 29A | 121 | 8 | 11-Dec-2007 | Spurlin |
| Tudor Les Robert | 27 | 30 | 3 | 5-May-1999 | Ramsey |
| Tudor Louise | 17 | 25 | 15 | 18-Oct-2004 | Ramsey |
| Tudor Lula | 29A | 121 | 7 | 20-Oct-2006 | Spurlin |
| Tudor Nell | 30 | 35 | 1 | 26-Aug-2003 | Spurlin |
| Tudor Roy | 33 | 16 | 8 | 25-May-2004 | Spurlin |
| Tuggle Rachel | 18 | 31 | 5 | 17-Aug-2010 | Spurlin |
| Turner A. James | 31 | 23 | 1 | 28-Dec-2009 | Spurlin |
| Turner B. Ezie | 16 | 10 | 7 | 14-Oct-2009 | Ramsey |
| Turner C. J. | 30 | 51 | 6 | 19-Sep-1996 | Ramsey |
| Turner Dan | 30 | 50 | 4 | 26-Jan-1999 | Ramsey |
| Turner Dorsie | 22 | 11 | 11 | 3-Feb-2009 | Spurlin |
| Turner Emma | 30 | 119 | 3 | 10-Nov-2006 | Ramsey |
| Turner Garner | 30 | 118 | 1 | 15-Jan-1999 | Ramsey |
| Turner Hazel | 30 | 51 | 5 | 14-Dec-2002 | Ramsey |
| Turner Ray | 16 | 56 | 13 | 22-Oct-1996 | Ramsey |

* Cremains buried at the foot of Grave #1

| Name | Sec | Lot | Grave | Interment Date | Director |
|------|-----|-----|-------|----------------|----------|
| Turner Robert | 22 | 11 | 12 | 20-Nov-1999 | Spurlin |
| Tuttle Flossie | 20 | 33A | 1 | 10-Apr-2006 | Ramsey |
| Tyree Frances | 21 | 30 | 8 | 9-Jul-2009 | Spurlin |
| Underwood Allen J. | 33 | 46 | 8 | 21-Feb-2000 | Stith |
| Underwood Jeff | 31 | 33 | 5 | 10-Mar-2003 | Ramsey |
| Underwood M. Anna | 30 | 98 | 7 | 8-May-2002 | Ramsey |
| Underwood Myrtie | 12 | 43 | 10 | 27-Aug-2001 | Preston Pruitt |
| Underwood Ralph | 23 | 35 | 8 | 19-Jun-2006 | Stith |
| Underwood Vina | 23 | 35 | 14 | 13-Nov-2004 | Preston Pruitt |
| Vance Holly | 20 | 43A | 17 | 12-May-2000 | Ramsey |
| Vanderpool Roxie | 30 | 111 | 3 | 16-May-2000 | Spurlin |
| Vaughn Cynthia | 30 | 125 | 7 | 21-May-1998 | Kerr Bros |
| Vaught Wade | 32 | 39 | 8 | 18-Apr-2003 | Spurlin |
| Vockery William | 29A | 41 | 2 | 20-Sep-2004 | Oldman |
| Votaw Billy | 30 | 13A | 1 | 3-Apr-1999 | Randsdall |
| Votaw Loretta | 33 | 62 | 1 | 30-Jan-2009 | Alexander |
| Wade Judy | 29A | 116 | 2 | 5-May-2008 | Stith |
| Wade Sue | 34 | 49 | 7 | 30-Jun-2008 | Stith |
| Waggner Judy | 33 | 27 | 5 | 19-Jul-1997 | Ramsey |
| Walker Caroline | 9 | 12 | 7 | 9-Jun-1995 | Ramsey |
| Walker Sarah | 30 | 76 | 1 | 7-Sep-2007 | Ramsey |
| Wall Frances | 21 | 9 | 15 | 3-Aug-2009 | Barnett |
| Wall Robert | 31 | 20 | 4 | 18-Oct-2008 | Spurlin |
| Wall Ruby | 30 | 180 | 5 | 15-Aug-2008 | Milward |
| Wall Stanley M. | 30 | 180 | 6 | 19-Jun-2007 | Milward |
| Walton Bernice | 27 | 22 | 9 | 17-Apr-1998 | Ramsey |

| Name | Sec | Lot | Grave | Interment Date | Director |
|---|---|---|---|---|---|
| Walton Doria | 23 | 30 | 14 | 8-Feb-2001 | Ramsey |
| Walton Gordon | 26 | 14 | 6 | 17-Dec-2009 | Ramsey |
| Walton Herbert | 23 | 30 | 15 | 29-Nov-1999 | Ramsey |
| Walton Homer | 30 | 18 | 8 | 15-Aug-2001 | Ramsey |
| Walton Kieth | 27 | 22 | 9 | 6-Aug-2010 | Ramsey |
| Walton Lucy | 26 | 12 | 9 | 4-Feb-2004 | Stith |
| Walton Marie | 26 | 14 | 7 | 16-Jul-2001 | Ramsey |
| Walton Naomi | 30 | 18 | 7 | 23-Aug-2002 | Ramsey |
| Walton R. Kenny II | 23 | 30 | 16 | 19-Aug-2008 | Spurlin |
| Walton T. J. | 27 | 35 | 14 | 22-Aug-2003 | Ramsey |
| Ward Ethel | 33 | 15 | 1 | 18-May-1996 | Ramsey |
| Wardlow Marjorie | 18 | 37 | 14 | 3-Feb-2010 | Spurlin |
| Warfield Martha | 34 | 49 | 3 | 12-Jan-2008 | Spurlin |
| Warmoth Jesse | 33 | 16 | 6 | 2-Oct-2006 | Ramsey |
| Warren Harold | 33 | 39 | 8 | 18-Dec-1998 | Ramsey |
| Warren Opal | 33 | 39 | 7 | 7-Sep-1998 | Ramsey |
| Watkins Adloph | 10 | 4 | 10 | 1-May-2006 | Ramsey |
| Watkins B. Lois | 11 | 31 | 14 | 14-Nov-2005 | Ramsey |
| Watkins Irene | 33 | 31 | 1 | 27-Feb-1996 | Ramsey |
| Watkins Margaret | 27 | 25 | 7 | 4-Jul-1997 | Spurlin |
| Watkins Virgie | 27 | 21 | 12 | 18-Oct-1996 | Ramsey |
| Watson Ralph | 30 | 45 | 2 | 13-Feb-2010 | Fox |
| Wearren Billy | 7 | 25 | 16 | 15-Dec-2003 | Ramsey |
| Webb Johnetta | 24 | 25 | 12 | 13-Nov-2002 | Ramsey |
| Weddle Margaret | 18 | 4 | 15 | 27-Mar-2010 | Kerr Bros |
| Wert James | 25 | 28 | 2 | 15-Jul-2006 | Stith |
| West Doris | 32 | 39 | 5 | 17-Jul-2003 | Spurlin |
| West John | 32 | 39 | 6 | 2-Apr-2001 | Spurlin |

| Name | Sec | Lot | Grave | Interment Date | Director |
|---|---|---|---|---|---|
| West Lucy | 29A | 104 | 5 | 18-Jan-2003 | Ramsey |
| West Mary | 30 | 9 | 1 | 19-Nov-2001 | Ramsey |
| West Ralph | 32 | 25 | 8 | 10-Dec-1998 | Ramsey |
| Whalen Alma | 24 | 22 | 4 | 5-Jan-2001 | Ramsey |
| Whalen Rose | 21 | 32 | 14 | 3-Jan-2008 | Spurlin |
| White Edna | 22 | 20 | 1 | 26-May-2005 | Ramsey |
| White Joe | 28 | 12 | 16 | 21-Apr-2001 | Ramsey |
| White John | 22 | 20 | 2 | 19-Feb-2009 | Ramsey |
| Whitehouse Ethel | 33 | 44 | 1 | 6-Dec-2000 | Wilder |
| Whitis Nora | 33 | 24 | 5 | 30-Aug-2005 | Ramsey |
| Whitis Virgil | 33 | 24 | 6 | 11-Aug-1995 | Ramsey |
| Whittaker Dorothy | 28 | 10 | 13 | 12-Jan-2008 | Combs |
| Whittaker Ella Lou | 18 | 3 | 14 | 21-Dec-2004 | Ramsey |
| Whittaker Fannie | 16 | 51 | 13 | 10-Apr-2009 | Spurlin |
| Whittaker Hazel | 21 | 32 | 15 | 20-Sep-1997 | Ramsey |
| Whittaker Margaret | 23 | | * | 11-Oct-1995 | Ramsey |
| Whittaker Marguerite | 22 | 15 | 5 | 24-Feb-2001 | Spurlin |
| Whittaker Marshall | 21 | 32 | 16 | 29-Jul-1998 | Ramsey |
| Whittaker Ruby | 21 | 32 | 6 | 16-Nov-2004 | Spurlin |
| Wilkins Aileen | 24 | 18 | 3 | 18-Feb-1997 | Spurlin |
| Williams Helen | 13 | 21 | 8 | 3-Nov-2006 | Ramsey |
| Williams Jerome | 33 | 18 | 2 | 23-Jan-2004 | Ramsey |
| Wilmot Ethel | 29A | 80 | 8 | 2-Oct-2007 | Ramsey |
| Wilson Jewell | 30 | 47 | 3 | 5-Jul-2006 | Spurlin |
| Wilson Norma | 22 | 8 | 2 | 8-Aug-2003 | Lazor |
| Wilson Shirley | 25 | 28 | 9 | 25-Jul-1997 | Ramsey |
| Wilson Stella | 25 | 28 | 14 | 1-Jun-2004 | Ramsey |
| Winchester Carolyn | 34 | 40 | 1 | 25-Aug-2004 | Ramsey |

* No Grave or Lot stated

| Name | Sec | Lot | Grave | Interment Date | Director |
|---|---|---|---|---|---|
| Winchester Eva | 33 | 40 | 6 | 24-Mar-1995 | Ramsey |
| Winchester Hubert | 33 | 40 | 7 | 9-Sep-2004 | Ramsey |
| Winchester Johnny | 34 | 40 | 2 | 15-Jun-2009 | Ramsey |
| Witt Bertha | 27 | 11 | 7 | 1-Dec-1999 | Spurlin |
| Witt Ollie | 27 | 11 | 6 | 12-Aug-1996 | Ramsey |
| Witt Onera | 27 | 11 | 15 | 8-Sep-2005 | Combs |
| Wood Cecil | 9 | 17 | 4 | 22-Apr-1996 | Stith |
| Woods Lanier | 19 | 24 | 16 | 8-Jun-1999 | Stith |
| Woods Leonard | 16 | 41 | 12 | 17-Mar-1998 | Ramsey |
| Woods Mary | 20 | 47 | 15 | 18-Mar-1996 | Ramsey |
| Woolcott Jane | 22 | 7 | 15 | 21-Jul-2000 | Milward |
| Wotorwise Pearl | 27 | 5 | 3&4 | 14-Nov-2004 | |
| Wren William | 33 | 38 | 8 | 27-Feb-1999 | Spurlin |
| Wright Ruth | 22 | 12 | 11 | 2-Mar-2001 | Ramsey |
| Wyler Fred | 23 | 7 | 12 | 9-Oct-2000 | Spurlin |
| Wylie Nora | 33 | 13 | 5 | 9-Aug-2010 | Spurlin |
| Wylie Vermill | 29A | 50 | 7 | 9-Apr-2002 | Ramsey |
| Wynn Lucille | 19 | 24 | 2 | 27-Dec-2004 | Heady |
| Yantis Mary | 29A | 102 | 1 | 25-Apr-1998 | Fox |
| Yeakey Cecil | 30 | 111 | 2 | 20-Feb-1999 | Ramsey |
| Yeakey David | 30 | 88 | 5 | 11-Jul-1995 | Ramsey |
| Yeakley Elvaree | 19 | 2 | 6 | 14-May-2001 | Ramsey |
| Young A. Julia | 30 | 94 | 3 | 26-Sep-2009 | Spurlin |
| Young C. Herman | 29A | 47 | 8 | 13-Mar-2000 | Ramsey |
| Young Ellen | 18 | 22 | 2 | 3-Feb-2000 | Spurlin |
| Young Helen | 29A | 47 | 7 | 3-Apr-2009 | Ramsey |
| Young Keeton Ruth | 33 | 57 | 3 | 10-Apr-2001 | Ramsey |
| Young Nora | 18 | 27 | 9 | 18-Aug-2005 | Ramsey |

| Name | Sec | Lot | Grave | Interment Date | Director |
|---|---|---|---|---|---|
| Young Paul | 18 | 27 | 10 | 14-Apr-2009 | Ramsey |
| Zanone Flossie | 16 | 28 | 10 | 26-Feb-2002 | Preston Pruitt |
| Zanone Jack | 29A | 122 | 4 | 28-Aug-2003 | Ramsey |
| Zanone Norma | 29A | 123 | 5 | 11-Mar-2009 | Spurlin |

# About Personal Touch Genealogy

J. L. Dickson and Personal Touch Genealogy offer research services to obtain public record documents from any of these Kentucky counties:

- Boyle
- Frankfort (State Archives)
- Garrard
- Jessamine (Documents Only)
- Lincoln
- Madison
- Rockcastle (Documents Only)
- Genealogy research in other counties available by request.

My professional services focus on customer service and satisfaction, and are based on years of quality training and experience.

Don't skimp on qualifications when you are looking for accuracy.

My credentials include:

- Genealogy Instructor and Family Archivist

- Taught by a genealogist with 45 years of professional experience for 3 years

- Positions held at genealogical and historical societies include Vice President, Board of Directors, Webmaster, Staff Genealogist, Archivist and Newsletter Editor

- Over a decade of experience working on my own personal research

- Listed as a Kentucky County Research Specialist by the Kentucky State Archives

- My main focus is documentation ... let the documents tell the story!

Visit my website at **www.PersonalTouchGenealogy.com** to learn more, or to contact me.

# ORDER FORM

Name _____

Address _____

City _____

State _____ ZIP _____

Area Code/Phone _____

Email _____

**Lancaster Cemetery, Garrard County, Kentucky
Interment Dates & Locations
1995-2010**

Quantity: _____ @ $25 each                    _____

Plus $5.00 shipping                                          _____

Kentucky residents add 6% for state sales tax     _____

                                        **TOTAL:**        _____

Bulk purchasing, shipping and handling quotes
available upon request.

Mail this form with your check or money order to:
J. L. Dickson
P. O. Box 333
Stanford, KY 40484

You may also order on our website
www.PersonalTouchGenealogy.com or
email us at personaltouch.genealogy@yahoo.com

www.ingramcontent.com/pod-product-compliance
Lightning Source LLC
Chambersburg PA
CBHW070931270326
41927CB00011B/2808